Book

"THE EMBODIMENT OF A KINGDOM WATCHMAN" is for anyone who desires to learn more about entering, asserting authority over, and conquering spiritual and natural realms. It is designed to broaden your revelation, anointing, and relationship with God and working as God's kingdom ambassador, while effectively governing and establishing His name and kingdom in your life and sphere of influence.

**KINGDOM SHIFTERS
EMBODIMEN OF A KINGDOM
WATCHMAN WARFARE MANUAL II**

TaquettaBaker@Kingdomshifters.com

(Website) Kingdomshifters.com

**Connect with Taquetta via Facebook or
YouTube**

Copyright 2014 – Kingdom Shifters Ministries

Taquetta's Bio

Taquetta Baker is the founder of Kingdom Shifters Ministries (KSM). She has authored fourteen books and two decree CD's. Taquetta has a Master's Degree in Community Counseling with an emphasis on Marriage, Children and Family Counseling, a Bachelor's Degree in Psychology and Associates Degree in Business Administration. In addition, Taquetta has a Therapon Belief Therapist Certification from Therapon Institute and has 22 years of professional and Christian Counseling experience.

Taquetta is also gifted at empowering and assisting people with launching ministries, businesses and books and provides mentoring, counseling and vision casting through Kingdom Shifters Kingdom Wellness Program.
Taquetta serves on the Board of Directors for New Day Community Ministries, Inc. of Muncie, IN. In October 2008, Taquetta graduated from the Eagles Dance Institute under Dr. Pamela Hardy and received her license in the area of liturgical dance. Before launching into her own ministry, Taquetta served at her previous church for 12 years. She was a prophet, pioneer and leader of Shekinah Expressions Dance Ministry, teacher, member of the presbytery board, and overseer of the Altar Workers Ministry. Taquetta receives mentoring and ministry covering from Bishop Jackie Green, Founder of JGM-National PrayerLife Institute (Phoenix, AZ), and was ordained as an Apostle on June 7, 2014.

Taquetta flows through the wells of warfare and worship and mantles an apostolic mandate of judging and establishing God's kingdom in people, ministries, communities, and regions. Taquetta travels in foreign missions and throughout the United States. She has *mentored and established dance, altar workers, deliverance, and prophetic ministries. Taquetta ministers in the areas of fine arts, all manners of prayer, fivefold ministry, deliverance, healing, miracles, atmospheric worship, and empowers and train people in their destiny and life's vision.*

Connect with Taquetta and KSM at <u>kingdomshifters.com</u> or via Facebook. For more information regarding Bishop Jackie Green at Jgmenternational.org.

Table Of Contents

FOREWORD

*"Embodiment of a Kingdom Watchman"
provides revelation and impartation to a prayer
warrior on how to discern, enter and assert
authority within the earth and the heavens. This
book births forth the fullness of who a
consecrated kingdom watchman should be in
their entirety. It provides insight, revelation,
and scriptural foundation on not only what you
should look like and do as a prayer warrior, but
what you can do to obtain it, how to shift
yourself into being in tune with God and the
Holy Spirit as a prayer warrior, how to release
glory, power, and authority as you pray
personally, as a ministry, in churches, over
regions, and for the world. This book is
expansive and does not limit God, but releases
unending revelation and impartation from His
limitless and unsearchable living word. The
reach of this book is indescribable as it does not
stop at just being a prayer warrior, but it steps
into helping its reader walk in calling, govern
and overtake realms, discern spirits, and being
personally accountable to God living a daily
lifestyle of repentance and cleansing. It holds the
entire package and will aid you in positioning
yourself to be a prayer warrior that is not only
effective and powerful, but pleasing and
honorable to God. This is the Embodiment of a
Prayer Warrior, God's Prayer Warrior!*

*Blessings,
Nina Cook,
Taquetta's Spiritual Daughter*

FOREWORD

*The good person out of the good treasure of (her)
heart produces good. (Lk 6:45a) This scripture I
feel best expresses what you now hold in your
hands. To know the author is to know a deep
watered well. A woman of forethought who not
only knows where she wants to go but couples
that with knowledge of how to get there. This
manual comes from a deep place within her and
has been paid for with tears, scars and
intercession.*

*From these elements you now hold what in some
ways may seem like a manifesto and manual but
in the end is the framework of a fresh movement
that is going forth throughout the earth from
those who hunger and thirst for righteousness in
our age. This book provides clarity to the inner
groanings of many and awakens the reader to
kingdom responsibility in pursuit of the
manifestation of the Father's will.*

*In many books you'll have an activation or
decree given with little to no explanation as to
why you are decreeing or praying the prayer. In
this book you are trained first and overwhelmed
with the depth of information before given the
opportunity to release the decree. By the time
you get to the decree it's already a part of you.
The words are broken down in the Greek and
Hebrew. They're listed and catalogued. This
way of wording and display begin to immerse
you into a picture of the revelation which allows
you to take it in on a personal level. From this,
you can practice the word and adjust it to meet*

your needs over time. It's definitely a different approach not to be overlooked.

In this book you will hear the heart of true intercession and worship. Taquetta has a desire and burden to release and equip many into such an anointing. In an age of wishy-washy and feel good first, this book comes like a voice crying out in the wilderness calling out to true lovers of God and demanding they systematically, indefinitely and irrevocably lay down their lives. So may you digest and enjoy the Embodiment of a Kingdom Watchman.
Prophet Noble Headley, Chicago, IL

FOREWORD

The Embodiment of A Kingdom Watchman by: Taquetta Baker is filled with powerful warfare insight and it covers a host of deliverance teaching coupled with, to me the most important principle of all a consecrated lifestyle.

Each chapter is filled with practical insight that can be put to use, I highly recommend this manual to be used for deliverance training classes.

The revelation of the Kingdom and Apostolic insight is well expressed in the Manual.

Apostle Ivory Hopkins

Founder of Pilgrims Ministry of Deliverance Georgetown Delaware

Chancellor of East Coast RDU Rapha Healing and Deliverance University

Purity Of A Kingdom Watchman

By: Nina Cook

Romans 12:1-2 - I appeal to you therefore, brethren, and beg of you in view of [all] the mercies of God, to make a decisive dedication of your bodies [presenting all your members and faculties] as a living sacrifice, holy (devoted, consecrated) and well pleasing to God, which is your reasonable (rational, intelligent) service and spiritual worship.

Do not be conformed to this world (this age), [fashioned after and adapted to its external, superficial customs], but be transformed (changed) by the [entire] renewal of your mind [by its new ideals and its new attitude], so that you may prove [for yourselves] what is the good and acceptable and perfect will of God, even the thing which is good and acceptable and perfect [in His sight for you].

As prayer warriors and Kingdom watchmen we have a call to purity. In order to be a fully effective Kingdom advancer, discerner, realm governor, possessor of God's nature and character, and releaser of God's glory, will and purposes, you have to aim to live a life committed and devoted to God that is free of contamination and compromise. From this scripture we learn that our call to

1

present our bodies as a living sacrifice, holy and acceptable to God is our service and spiritual worship. Purity is a part of our presentation to God. When we are praying, entering and taking authority in the earthly and heavenly realms, aiming to discern people, churches, and regions, flow with the Holy Spirit and etc. we have to present ourselves in order to obtain and operate in these things. And if we are not presentable and pure before God this will hinder our ability, effectiveness, and flow in each of these areas. The enemy can and will use areas of impurity, compromise, and ongoing sin to accuse, oppose and resist us.

The scripture then further states, *to not be conformed to this world, but be transformed by the renewal of your mind.* In our pursuit of purity we have to live a lifestyle of daily mind renewal. In doing so, we follow hard after the perfect will of God and understand what is good and acceptable to Him. Not what is good, acceptable, and morally right to our families, friends, or in our cultural and world systems; but what does God require of us in our service of purity and holiness. This is what we have to meditate and feast upon such that we are consistently transformed by it and in alignment with it. By walking in this level of constant and ever

2

going transformation no matter what is going on around we can stand strong, boldly and unwaveringly in God standards.

One way to pursue and maintain a life of purity is through spending time reading and mediating, embracing, ingesting, and then mirroring the word of God. In life in general the more time you spend with someone, the more you begin to know them and sometimes you may even sound or do things like them without you even noticing. God's word is pure and holy, light releasing, and living. So as you spend time in God's word you will begin to know what He deems pure and holy (get to know God), and then you can absorb and put on its holiness, purity, and light (begin to do things like God). As you ingest God's word, it becomes a part of you, and drives out what opposes it. The word itself goes to work in you and purges you out of all that does not reflect God's pure and holy nature.

Psalms 119:140 - Thy word is very pure: therefore thy servant loveth it.

Proverbs 30:5 - Every word of God is pure: he is a shield unto them that put their trust in him.

Psalms 33:4 - For the word of the Lord is right; and all his works are done in truth.

Psalms 119:105 - Thy word is a lamp unto my feet, and a light unto my path.

Joshua 1:8 - This book of the law shall not depart out of thy mouth; but thou shalt meditate therein day and night, that thou mayest observe to do according to all that is written therein: for then thou shalt make thy way prosperous, and then thou shalt have good success.

Psalms 1:2 - But his delight is in the law of the Lord; and in his law doth he meditate day and night.

Hebrews 4:12 states: *For the Word that God speaks is alive and full of power [making it active, operative, energizing, and effective]; it is sharper than any two-edged sword, penetrating to the dividing line of the breath of life (soul) and [the immortal] spirit, and of joints and marrow [of the deepest parts of our nature], exposing and sifting and analyzing and judging the very thoughts and purposes of the heart.*

Living a daily life in pursuit of purity through embodying and mirroring the word of God positions you in a place to continually have the deepest parts of your nature, soul and spirit divided, sifted, and analyzed by the Spirit of God in what is of Him and what is not of Him. If there are any areas of impurity, ongoing sin, error,

4

unconscious ungodly thoughts, behaviors and etc. the spirit of God whom searches all things will find it and discern it and penetrate and purify your thoughts and purposes.

1Corinthians 2:10 - But God hath revealed them unto us by his Spirit: for the Spirit searcheth all things, yea, the deep things of God.

By allowing God's Spirit and word to purify and search you, you cancel any chance of mixture. The Spirit is perfect and will search all things, the deep things of God leaving nothing to linger and fester. By surrendering to the inner searching and working of the Spirit you also release yourself of all striving and self-perfection and you relinquish trust in God to consistently cleanse you and lead you in your call to purity.

John 1:1 - In the beginning was the Word, and the Word was with God, and the Word was God.

John 1:14 - And the Word was made flesh, and dwelt among us, (and we beheld his glory, the glory as of the only begotten of the Father,) full of grace and truth.

Jesus was the word, and we too have to be the word and embody it, demonstrate it, and allow it to be displayed and established in us. Jesus was flawless in His ability to walk out His destiny and purposes because He was the very word and will of God. He held the glory and the fullness of God in the very essence of His being, and was perfect in knowing what was of God and what was not. Jesus lived a life of total purity. We must allow the word of God to become flesh in us and dwell within us. By allowing Gods word to become flesh in you, you allow it to purify you and change your nature to that of the nature of God. You then hold the word in your members and now have the ability to hold true to it, and embody it as Jesus did.

Psalms 24:1-5 - The earth is the Lord's, and the fulness thereof; the world, and they that dwell therein. For he hath founded it upon the seas, and established it upon the floods. Who shall ascend into the hill of the Lord? Or who shall stand in his holy place? He that hath clean hands, and a pure heart; who hath not lifted up his soul unto vanity, nor sworn deceitfully. He shall receive the blessing from the Lord, and righteousness from the God of his salvation.

Possessing purity is a key that will allow us the ability to ascend into the hill of the Lord and stand in His holy place. We are seated in heavenly places with Christ, but in order to receive the fullness of this truth and blessing we have to have clean hands and a pure heart to ascend and stand in the holy places of the Lord. In the scripture the Lord is informing us that He owns everything (*the earth is the Lord's and the fullness thereof; the world, and they that dwell therein*), and because He owns everything, if we have clean hands and pure hearts we will receive blessings from Him and be granted the ability to ascend and stand in His holy place. That is entrance and authority over all the heavens and the earth.

With purity as prayer warriors we will always have unlimited access into the realms of earth and heaven, thus increasing our authority, reign and rule there. Also increasing our spiritual accuracy, excellence, and discernment, and increase our exposure, and ownership; while allowing us to walk in the blessings of being co-heirs with Christ and having dominion and rule in the earth and heaven.

Keys to Purity of a Kingdom Watchman:

- Understand that you have a call to purity, and have the mindset that it is service and spiritual worship to the Lord (it is pleasing to God)
- Live a life committed and devoted to God that is free of contamination and compromise
- Understand that purity is a part of your presentation. As a prayer warrior presentation is key as you go in and out of the spiritual realm. The enemy can use your presentation against you, and it can hinder you in being an effective prayer warrior
- Follow hard after the perfect will of God, and know what is good and acceptable to Him
- Meditate on what is good and acceptable to Him such that it can consistently transform you and become a part of your normal standard
- Spend time reading, meditating, embracing, ingesting, and then mirroring the word of God. Let the word transform and change you
- Absorb God's word and put on its holiness, purity, and light
- Allow God's Spirit and word to search, sift and analyze you, it is true and perfect and

will not lead you astray or return unto you void. It will purify and transform you. You will see fruit

- Be open and willing to pray on what the Spirit of God reveals to you as far as impurities, ongoing sin, compromise, and etc.
- Allow the word to be made flesh in you, let it be established in all of your members as you pursue to become the very will, and purposes of God

Armored Up!

In *Ephesians 6:13-17*, we see the armor needed for a prayer warrior aka kingdom watchman.

New International Version
Be strong in the Lord and in his mighty power. Put on the full armour of God so that you can take your stand against the devil's schemes. For our struggle is not against flesh and blood, but against the rulers, against the authorities, against the powers of this dark world and against the spiritual forces of evil in the heavenly realms. Therefore put on the full armour of God, so that when the day of evil comes, you may be able to stand your ground, and after you have done everything, to stand.

*Stand firm then, with the **belt of truth buckled** round your waist, with the **breastplate of righteousness** in place, and with your feet fitted with the readiness that comes from the **gospel of peace**. In addition to all this, take up the **shield of faith**, with which you can extinguish all the flaming arrows of the evil one. Take the **helmet of salvation** and the **sword of the Spirit**, which is the word of God.*

This is literal armor that we should never take off, as our warfare armor represents the very character and nature of God. We are wearing His essence and in doing so we are able to assert authority over the enemy.

Other scriptures that reveal the armored character and nature of God needed to combat the enemy are as follows:

Galatians 5:22-23 - *But the fruit of the Spirit is love, joy, peace, longsuffering, gentleness, goodness, faith, meekness, temperance: against such there is no law.*

The Message Version - *But what happens when we live God's way? He brings gifts into our lives, much the same way that fruit appears in an orchard—things like affection for others, exuberance about life, serenity. We develop a willingness to stick with things, a sense of compassion in the heart, and a conviction that a basic holiness permeates things and people. We find ourselves involved in loyal commitments, not needing to force our way in life, able to marshal and direct our energies wisely. Legalism is helpless in bringing this about; it only gets in the way.*

Matthew 7:15-20 - *Beware of false prophets, which come to you in sheep's clothing, but inwardly they are ravening wolves. Ye shall know them by their fruits. Do men gather grapes of thorns, or figs of thistles? Even so every good tree bringeth forth good fruit; but a corrupt tree bringeth forth evil fruit. A good tree cannot bring forth evil fruit, neither can a corrupt tree bring forth good fruit. Every tree that bringeth not forth good fruit is hewn down, and cast into the fire. Wherefore by their fruits ye shall know them.*

11

Sheep's clothing is the garment of Satan. God's nature and character aka "*fruits*" is the garment of God. When we are bearing fruit, we are displaying our orientation and reflecting God, while producing and reproducing His fruit in the earth. God's fruit is the armor that proclaims we are not Satan's. We are in the army of the Most High God.

Once armored in God, we are able to contend with the wiles of the enemy.

Ephesians 6-10-12 - Finally, my brethren, be strong in the Lord, and in the power of his might. Put on the whole armour of God, that ye may be able to stand against the wiles of the devil. For we wrestle not against flesh and blood, but against principalities, against powers, against the rulers of the darkness of this world, against spiritual wickedness in high places.

The wiles of the enemy are as follows:

- *Principalities* are satanic princes and territorial spirits ruling over a nation, city, region, and community for the purposes of establishing Satan's demonic plan in people's lives and spheres.
- *Powers* are high ranking supernatural demons or demonic influences that cause evil and sin in the world.
- *Rulers of Darkness* are demonic forces that govern deception and manipulative

12

hardships and catastrophes that are generally produced by witchcraft, manipulation of the weather and worldly systems; they operate in cultures and countries such that idolatry and sin rein in the earth.

- *Spiritual Wickedness in High Places* are evil plots and deceptions, and demonic attacks directed in and against the church and God's people for the purposes of hindering, contaminating and demolishing God's will in the earth.
- *Strongholds* are demonic possession or depression; demonic grip, harassment, influences, or hindrance that prevents a person from being free to walk in the full salvation for the Lord.

As you eternally wear God's armored fruit, these noticeable characteristics should manifest.

Nature & Character Of A Prayer Warrior
Dedicated
Reliable
Integral
Empathetic
Compassionate
Objective
Balanced
Loving & kind
Forgiving
Pursuer of deliverance and healing
Holy Spirit lead
Mindset of Christ

Obedient
Discerning
Disciplined
A leader
Administrative
A team player
Empowering of others
High moral character
Teachable
Constant learner
Operate in the Gift of Faith
Risk taker
Supernatural

The rest of this chapter is written from the revelation and notes Reenita Keys, my spiritual daughter, received when studying the armor of God and reading the book entitled, "*The Complete Armor of God (spiritual warfare for end time warriors).*"

Ephesians 6:14-19
Stand therefore, having fastened on the belt of truth, and having put on the breastplate of righteousness, and, as shoes for your feet, having put on the readiness given by the gospel of peace. In all circumstances take up the shield of faith, with which you can extinguish all the flaming darts of the evil one; and take the helmet of salvation, and the sword of the Spirit, which is the word of God, praying at all times in the Spirit, with all prayer and supplication. To that end keep alert with all perseverance, making supplication for all the saints, and also for me, that words may be given to me in opening my

mouth boldly to proclaim the mystery of the gospel.

Defensive Armor:

You have to remember that the armor is not yours but it is God's armor. Kings would send out their best champion to fight in their armor. The victory would be given to the king and not the person that was fighting in the battle. This revelation puts us in rememberance of how God made Saul's armor uncomfortable and unfitting for David *(1Samuel 17:38-40)*. It would have been a cool thing to wear King Saul's armor but it is more important to be armored in who we are in God. David was God's champion not Saul's. When we put on the kings armor we are fighting the king's enemies. So when we put on the armor OF GOD, His enemies become our enemies.

The waist belt of truth protects our emotions and keeps us from the lies of the enemy. In the old times, God's people believed that the waist area was where our emotions manifested, as opposed to our emotions from the heart. When we put on the belt of truth we are wrapping ourselves in the truth of God. With being wrapped in God's truth, we are able to make the devil flee from us easier. This also allows us to not succumb to emotional responses and lies of the devil.

The breastplate protects the lungs and the heart. This is where our Spirit is. In the Hebrew Holy Spirit is called *"pneuma,"* and means breath of God. The Lord wants to protect the lungs because this is where He breathes life. The enemy will come and try to accuse us because we can't obtain righteousness outside of Jesus. When we accept Jesus Christ, His righteousness protects us from lies. If the enemy were to go to God to accuse us, it would be pointless because God knows everything we do, right and wrong. God knows us inside and out. It would be like someone going to your dad and telling him that you are not his child and telling him different things about you even though your father already knows you are his child, and knows you like the back of his hand. Instead of going to the father, the accuser would rather go to the child and tell them that their father is not their father or that their father does not really love them. Through righteousness we are protected from these tricks of the enemy. Any accusation is protected by the breastplate of righteousness from God.

The shoes are what we stand on. The shoes of peace include the foundation of love and walking in salvation daily. God is the rock of our salvation that we stand on.

The shield of faith protects us from attacks sent from the enemy. The more we use our shield the bigger it grows. *James 2:20*

16

contends that faith without works is dead. The more we exercise our faith or shield of faith, the bigger and more powerful it becomes, almost like a muscle growing as we exercise it daily. Our shield of faith is now better able to come to our defense against the enemy. If we do not use our shield of faith, it becomes weak and useless.

The helmet of our salvation is to protect our thoughts and intellect. It protects the knowledge, while enabling us to come against every thought that tries to exalt itself against God in our lives. The enemy will try to send thoughts to pull us from our relationship with God. If he can attack our mind he is able to hinder the flow of the Holy Spirit. The Holy Spirit holds all knowledge of the things of God and allows us to overflow with the thoughts and plans of the Lord. If we do not protect our knowledge, we can come under attack by the things that are not of God.

The final defensive armor we have is the sword. So many people think of the sword of the Spirit as something that is used offensively in battle, however, this is in fact a part of our offensive armor as well. Offensively the sword of the spirit is a weapon and defensively the sword of the spirit is a part of our armor. Back in Paul's days the soldiers were taught how to protect themselves from spears and swords from the opposing team with their sword.

This would enable them to not only protect themselves from damage or being cut by their enemy. They could also counter attack with their sword. The sword is very important because it is a piece of armor that we can aim towards wherever the attack is coming from, block, and attack back.

We have to keep in mind that none of this armor is ours, but it belongs to the Lord. We are wearing it as God's sent ones. He gives us His armor and it forms to our body so we operate accurately and precisely with each movement in battle. When we enter the battle of warfare, because we are clothed in the armor of God, the enemy should not see us but see the Father. God gets all the glory and the victory belongs to the Lord. Through our armor we are inside the body, nature, character, plan of God, and He is activated as our strength, source of power, and shield.

The Amplified Version of Psalm 18:2 says:
The Lord is my Rock, my Fortress, and my Deliverer; my God, my keen and firm Strength in Whom I will trust and take refuge, my Shield, and the Horn of my salvation, my High Tower.

God is our rock which is the foundation we grounded in. This makes me think of the shoes that are a part of the armor. We stand on the rock of salvation and our shoes are infused with the gospel of peace. The reason I keep saying shoes and not saying

18

boots is because even though God may give us various boots for battle we should not limit him to boots. He may give us Nike's, tap dancing shoes, ballet slippers or shoes we've never even heard of or seen before. This is why it is strategic and important to put on your armor daily and envision what you are putting on, because the armor may change and things will definitely be added depending on the season, assignment and battle you are preparing for.

The scripture speaks further about God being our fortress. Usually when one thinks of a fortress, it is a huge structure designed to stand against impact. The fortress can be the secret place, but it is also a part of the armor of God. We are rising and standing on the fortress of God because we have on His armor. God's armor is not cheap or cheaply made and neither are we. God's armor is indestructible and we eternally live inside His armor. If we do not have this mindset before - in - after the battle, we are degrading who God is and who we are in Him.

The fortress can be viewed as a mobile shield like the shield of faith we possess. Can you imagine fighting and with every missile, shot fired, arrow thrown, and attack sent your way, this huge wall coming out of nowhere guarding you from those attacks. It makes me laugh because I can just see the faces of the opposing team frustrated and sad because we are advancing the Kingdom and their attacks are pointless.

The scripture expresses further that God is our deliverer. God is a deliverer and He never holds back anything from His children. When it comes to armor and spiritual warfare, God will deliver an abundant amount of weapons and upgrades to our armor. In the Spirit we will never run out of bullets, bows, arrows, missiles, battery life, gas for jets, or bombs because God will always deliver. God equips us with weapons we cannot even fathom. We should never lack or be without because we are hooked to Jehovah Jireh, the Lord our provider.

Psalm 18:2 also states that God is *our keen and firm strength in whom we can trust and take refuge. He is our Shield, the Horn of our salvation, our High Tower.*

We have to be keen and firm in the strength of God - not in your momma, brother, sister, cousin, best friend or associate. Discern and be keen in the Spirit. God trusts us to put on His armor. He trusts us not to use it for evil. We therefore have to trust and take refuge in our armor. He is the horn of our salvation, which could represent Him calling out our name wanting us to follow His voice and taking action regarding what He shares. This is why Psalms 27:4 says that the *deep cries out to the deep*. In the natural many have experienced their parent or guardian calling their name. Even if you were down the street it was almost as if your ears perked up and you went running home to see why you were being requested. We are keen to the Father's voice and can hear Him when He calls us by name. He called us and we answered this call of salvation when we gave our life to Christ. The call did not stop when we gave our life to Christ! This calling is constant, and as we diligently run towards His voice, we are being made to look like Jesus just by constantly answering. Jesus never ignored the call. And just like Jesus, we should be quick to listen, and heed the call, and be slow to speak.

James 1:19 - *Understand [this], my beloved brethren. Let every man be quick to hear [a ready listener], slow to speak, slow to take offense and to get angry.*

We have to listen and allow God to give us the blueprints of His armor. Someone who interrupts someone when they are talking will find that all the answers to the questions they have will be answered if they are slow to speak. If you are given a piece of armor that you do not understand do not take offense or get frustrated. Seek God for revelation and knowledge. Even if the revelation is not given right away, there may be a strategic plan God is giving you. For example, you may have to fast from certain things so that whatever is blocking the message God is trying to deliver can flow to your heart and be imparted into your Spirit.

Armor Activation:
- Seek the Lord in prayer and pray *Ephesians 6:14-19*. As you go before God envision yourself putting each piece of armor on and allow God to give you the revelation of each piece, what it means, what it is for, what it does and how you will use it.
- After you receive this, ask the Lord how you are to activate your armor. Take your time with each piece so you are quick to listen and slow to speak and not rushing the Holy Spirit.
- Write down or record everything God speaks and declare it forth.

Kingdom Discernment

Discernment in the Greek language means *judicial estimation, discern, disputation.* It comes from a word meaning *to separate thoroughly, withdraw, oppose, discriminate, decide, hesitate, contend, make to differ, doubt, judge, be partial, stagger, waver.*

If you are one who tends to wrestle with wavering in what you discern, then it is probably because God really wants you to pay attention to what He is revealing to you. When someone is operating in discernment, they are challenged by a person, matter or inkling that appears okay in the natural or on the outside, but something is not quite right on the inside or in the Spirit. The person discerning may experience the process described in the definition to get to the truth of what is being discerned. Discernment at times, is an inward war, where a person is striving to align what they perceive, with Who God is, and what is being offered.

1John 4:1 - Beloved, believe not every spirit, but try the spirits whether they are of God: because many false prophets are gone out into the world.

Hebrews 4:12 - For the word of God [is] quick, and powerful, and sharper than any twoedged sword, piercing even to the dividing asunder of soul and spirit, and of the joints and marrow, and [is] a discerner of the thoughts and intents of the heart.

Kingdom discernment requires relationship and sensitivity to God and His presence - Holy Spirit.

A person has to be sensitive to
1. How God feels
2. How God thinks
3. How God sees
4. How God judges
5. How God behaves
6. What God hears
7. What God believes
8. What pleases God
9. What God judges
10. God's purposes for mankind, His church, & the world

Our five natural senses have to be spiritually in tune with the nature, character, and plan of God for people, ministry, the region, and even the world at large.

1. Sight
2. Hearing
3. Touch
4. Smell
5. Taste

- *Nature* is the reality and disposition of who God is; how God acts, thinks, or behaves. It is the essence of who God is.
- *Character* is the attributes that make up who God is. It is what makes up God's nature.
- *Plan* is God's strategies, methods, schemes, for a particular people, place, or matter

Let us look at how our senses should work with God:

Sight
Ephesians 1:18 - *The eyes of your understanding being enlightened; that ye may know what is the hope of his calling, and what the riches of the glory of his inheritance in the saints.*

Job 42:5 - *I have heard of thee by the hearing of the ear: but now mine eye seeth thee.*

Hear
Proverbs 2:1-9 - *My son, if thou wilt receive my words, and hide my commandments with thee; So that thou incline thine ear unto wisdom, and apply thine heart to understanding; Yea, if thou criest after knowledge, and liftest up thy voice for understanding; If thou seekest her as silver, and searchest for her as for hid treasures; Then shalt thou understand the fear of the Lord, and find the knowledge of God. For the Lord giveth wisdom: out of his mouth cometh knowledge and understanding. He layeth up*

sound wisdom for the righteous: he is a buckler to them that walk uprightly. He keepeth the paths of judgment, and preserveth the way of his saints. Then shalt thou understand righteousness, and judgment, and equity; yea, every good path.

The Message Version - *Make Insight Your Priority Good friend, take to heart what I'm telling you; collect my counsels and guard them with your life. Tune your ears to the world of Wisdom; set your heart on a life of Understanding. That's right—if you make Insight your priority, and won't take no for an answer, Searching for it like a prospector panning for gold, like an adventurer on a treasure hunt, Believe me, before you know it Fear-of- God will be yours; you'll have come upon the Knowledge of God.*

And here's why: God gives out Wisdom free, is plainspoken in Knowledge and Understanding. He's a rich mine of Common Sense for those who live well, a personal bodyguard to the candid and sincere. He keeps his eye on all who live honestly, and pays special attention to his loyally committed ones. So now you can pick out what's true and fair, find all the good trails! Lady Wisdom will be your close friend, and Brother Knowledge your pleasant companion.

Proverbs 20:20-2 - *My son, attend to my words; incline thine ear unto my sayings. Let them not depart from thine eyes; keep them in the midst of thine heart. For they are life unto those that find them, and health to all their flesh.*

26

Keep thy heart with all diligence; for out of it are the issues of life.

Romans 10:17 - *Consequently, faith comes from hearing the message, and the message is heard through the word about Christ.*

Job 26:14 - *And these are but the outer fringe of his works; how faint the whisper we hear of him! Who then can understand the thunder of his power?"*

John 10:27 - *My sheep hear my voice, and I know them, and they follow me:*

Touch
Psalms 144:5 - *Bow thy heavens, O Lord, and come down: touch the mountains, and they shall smoke.*

Matthew 14:39 - *And besought him that they might only touch the hem of his garment: and as many as touched were made perfectly whole.*

Luke 6:19 - *And the whole multitude sought to touch him: for there went virtue out of him, and healed them all.*

Isaiah 11:2 - *The Spirit of the LORD will rest on him-- the Spirit of wisdom and of understanding, the Spirit of counsel and of might, the Spirit of the knowledge and fear of the LORD.*

1Samuel 10:26 - *And Saul also went home to Gibeah; and there went with him a band of men, whose hearts God had touched.*

Hebrews 4:15 - *For we have not an high priest which cannot be touched with the feeling of our infirmities; but was in all points tempted like as we are, yet without sin.*

Smell
2Corinthians 2:14 - *For we are unto God a sweet savour of Christ, in them that are saved, and in them that perish:*

Songs of Solomon 1:3 - *Pleasing is the fragrance of your perfumes; your name is like perfume poured out. No wonder the young women love you!*

Ezekiel 20:41 - *I will accept you as fragrant incense when I bring you out from the nations and gather you from the countries where you have been scattered, and I will be proved holy through you in the sight of the nations.*

Genesis 8:21 - *And the LORD smelled a sweet savour; and the LORD said in his heart, I will not again curse the ground any more for man's sake; for the imagination of man's heart is evil from his youth; neither will I again smite any more everything living, as I have done.*

Taste
Psalms 34:8 - *O taste and see that the LORD is good: blessed is the man that trusteth in him.*

Psalms 119:103 - *How sweet are your words to my taste, sweeter than honey to my mouth!*

Hebrews 5:4-5 - *For it is impossible for those who were once enlightened, and have tasted of the heavenly gift, and were made partakers of the Holy Ghost, and have tasted the good word of God, and the powers of the world to come.*

As revealed through the scriptures, all our senses overlap in some manner, such that if we did not hear God we should taste Him. If we do not see Him, we should hear Him. If we do not smell Him we should feel His touch. Unless God orchestrates it or we are in a level of sin that has caused dullness or death to our senses, there should never be a time that we cannot exercise discernment. And even then, we should possess a knowing that He has shielded us in this fashion.

We cannot discern other people, atmospheres, and regions until we:
- *Have cultivated a relationship with God*

Psalms 4:3 - *But know that the LORD hath set apart him that is godly for himself: the LORD will hear when I call unto him.*

Psalms 65:4 - *Blessed are those you choose and bring near to live in your courts! We are filled with the good things of your house, of your holy temple.*

- *Have discerned and gained significant authority over his or her own life, family, atmosphere, ministry, region*

Proverbs 20:27 - *The spirit of man is the candle of the Lord, searching all the inward parts of the belly.*

2Corinthians 3:18 - *But we all, with unveiled face, beholding as in a mirror the glory of the Lord, are being transformed into the same image from glory to glory, just as from the Lord, the Spirit.*

- **Have the heart of God (His heart encompasses His nature, character & plans)**

1Samuel 16:17 - *But the LORD said to Samuel, "Do not look at his appearance or at the height of his stature, because I have rejected him; for God sees not as man sees, for man looks at the outward appearance, but the LORD looks at the heart.*

1Corinthians 2:16 - *For who has known or understood the mind (the counsels and purposes) of the Lord so as to guide and instruct Him and give Him knowledge? But we have the mind of Christ (the Messiah) and do hold the thoughts (feelings and purposes) of His heart.*

When we discern through our natural senses, we are discerning through our instincts and intuitions. These are good attributes but can sway us as the natural part of us cannot discern what is of God and what is not of Him.

Ephesians 5:1-10

Be ye therefore followers of God, as dear children; And walk in love, as Christ also hath loved us, and hath given himself for us an offering and a sacrifice to God for a sweet-smelling savour. But fornication, and all uncleanness, or covetousness, let it not be once named among you, as becometh saints; neither filthiness, nor foolish talking, nor jesting, which are not convenient: but rather giving of thanks. For this ye know, that no whoremonger, nor unclean person, nor covetous man, who is an idolater, hath any inheritance in the kingdom of Christ and of God.

Let no man deceive you with vain words: for because of these things cometh the wrath of God upon the children of disobedience. Be not ye therefore partakers with them. For ye were sometimes darkness, but now are ye light in the Lord: walk as children of light: (For the fruit of the Spirit is in all goodness and righteousness and truth); Proving what is acceptable unto the Lord.

Proving in the Greek is *"dokimo"* and means, *"test, examine, prove, scrutinize, discern."*

Verse 10 The Message Version - *Figure out what will please Christ, and then do it.*

The Amplified Version - *And try to learn [in your experience] what is pleasing to the Lord [let your lives be constant proofs of what is most acceptable to Him].*

The natural senses tend to discern through what can be seen, understood, accepted as truth and tends to possess a self-focused benefit and motive. The natural senses tend to discern through what feels good, looks good, and what is desired *(lust of the eyes, lust of the flesh, and prides of life)*. Many people have a keen sense of natural discernment by which they detect conditions, but this is not discerning by the Spirit. As a result the natural discerner may think that what is of the natural is of God and be mistaken. Natural discernment fails when it comes to the great mysteries of the spiritual realm. *"The natural man receiveth not the things of the Spirit," for they are spiritually discerned."*

Let's explore natural discernment by considering the story of Isaac blessing Jacob instead of Esau.

Genesis 27:18-29
And he came unto his father, and said, my father: and he said, Here am I; who art thou, my son? And Jacob said unto his father, I am Esau thy firstborn; I have done according as thou badest me: arise, I pray thee, sit and eat of my venison, that thy soul may bless me. And Isaac said unto his son, how is it that thou hast found

32

it so quickly, my son? And he said, because the Lord thy God brought it to me. And Isaac said unto Jacob, Come near, I pray thee, that I may feel thee, my son, whether thou be my very son Esau or not. And Jacob went near unto Isaac his father; and he felt him, and said, the voice is Jacob's voice, but the hands are the hands of Esau. And he discerned him not, because his hands were hairy, as his brother Esau's hands: so he blessed him.

And he said, Art thou my very son Esau? And he said, I am. And he said, Bring it near to me, and I will eat of my son's venison, that my soul may bless thee. And he brought it near to him, and he did eat: and he brought him wine, and he drank. And his father Isaac said unto him, Come near now, and kiss me, my son. And he came near, and kissed him: and he smelled the smell of his raiment, and blessed him, and said, See, the smell of my son is as the smell of a field which the Lord hath blessed: Therefore God give thee of the dew of heaven, and the fatness of the earth, and plenty of corn and wine: Let people serve thee, and nations bow down to thee: be lord over thy brethren, and let thy mother's sons bow down to thee: cursed be every one that curseth thee, and blessed be he that blesseth thee.

Jacob discerned through natural senses of what felt and tasted good. He discerned through his desire. Though his spiritual senses kept cautioning him, it felt like Esau, smelled naturally like Esau, and because Jacob did not have his natural sense of sight to help him fully discern, He allowed himself to trust in his natural processing. This resulted in Jacob blessing the wrong son. He ended up passing down the families' rulership to the wrong son.

1Corinthians 2:14-16
The Amplified Version - *But the natural, nonspiritual man does not accept or welcome or admit into his heart the gifts and teachings and revelations of the Spirit of God, for they are folly (meaningless nonsense) to him; and he is incapable of knowing them [of progressively recognizing, understanding, and becoming better acquainted with them] because they are spiritually discerned and estimated and appreciated.*

But the spiritual man tries all things [he examines, investigates, inquires into, questions, and discerns all things], yet is himself to be put on trial and judged by no one [he can read the meaning of everything, but no one can properly discern or appraise or get an insight into him]. For who has known or understood the mind (the counsels and purposes) of the Lord so as to guide and instruct Him and give Him knowledge? But we have the mind of Christ (the Messiah) and do hold the thoughts (feelings and purposes) of His heart.

The Message Version - *The unspiritual self, just as it is by nature, can't receive the gifts of God's Spirit. There's no capacity for them. They seem like so much silliness. Spirit can be known only by spirit--God's Spirit and our spirits in open communion. Spiritually alive, we have access to everything God's Spirit is doing, and can't be judged by unspiritual critics. Isaiah's question, "Is there anyone around who knows God's Spirit, anyone who knows what he is doing?" has been answered: Christ knows, and we have Christ's Spirit.*

As we develop relationship with God, are consistent discerners of ourselves and our own sphere of influence, possess mature understanding of God's nature, character and plans through the treasures of His heart, then we can branch out to being pure discerners over other people, atmospheres and regions.

1Kings 3:9 - *Give therefore thy servant an understanding heart to judge thy people that I may discern between good and bad: for who is able to judge this thy so great a people?*

The Message Version - *Here's what I want: Give me a God- listening heart so I can lead your people well, discerning the difference between good and evil. For who on their own is capable of leading your glorious people?*

Understanding is "*sama*" in the Hebrew and means:

1. to hear intelligently, powerfully, judicially, soundly,
2. to hear, listen, and obey; to discern

35

Heart in the Hebrew is _"leb"_ and means:

1. the heart (as the most interior organ), the breast

2. comfortably, courage, ((faint), (tender-) heart ((- ed)), midst, mind, x unawares, understanding.

3. inner man, mind, will, heart, soul, understanding inner part, midst

4. midst (of things), heart (of man) soul, heart (of man) mind,

5. knowledge, thinking, reflection, memory,

6. inclination, resolution, determination (of will) conscience,

7. heart (of moral character) as seat of appetites, as seat of emotions and passions, as seat of courage

Solomon was asking for the ability to filter good and evil so he could lead the people properly. The only way he could do that was with an understanding heart which is the heart of God. The heart of God would enable Him to know what was important to God, what God's nature character and plan was, and then discern accordingly. In God's heart discerning comes down to being able to weigh information as good or bad, positive or negative, right or wrong, true or false, righteous or unrighteous, Godly or ungodly. There is no in between. A person or matter is either guilty or innocent, hot or cold. We may try to be lukewarm, but God does not deem something that is lukewarm of value.

Revelations 3:15-17 -The Amplified Version
I know your [record of] works and what you are doing; you are neither cold nor hot. Would that you were cold or hot! So, because you are lukewarm and neither cold nor hot, I will spew you out of My mouth! For you say, I am rich; I have prospered and grown wealthy, and I am in need of nothing; and you do not realize and understand that you are wretched, pitiable, poor, blind, and naked.

The Message Version
I know you inside and out, and find little to my liking. You're not cold, you're not hot––far better to be either cold or hot! You're stale. You're stagnant. You make me want to vomit. You brag, 'I'm rich, I've got it made, I need nothing from anyone,' oblivious that in fact you're a pitiful, blind beggar, threadbare and homeless.

God wants it clear what is of Him and what is not of Him. Therefore the power to discern resides in the ability to make a judicial decision that something is of Him and something is not of Him. That requires having God's heart and being obedient to what He states is profane or holy.

The reason I say this is because if we do not possess the heart of God then we tend to have mixture in our ability to discern. We will allow our opinions, critical perceptions, personal quirks, pet peeves, issues, experiences, and even what we think and feel about someone or a matter to intertwine with our ability to discern. Having God's heart keeps our heart, opinions, and critical perceptions under subjection. We are able to remain in the purity and keenness of discerning based on right or wrong, Godly versus ungodly, and based on God's standards rather than our own.

Psalms 75:7 - But God is the judge: he putteth down one, and setteth up another

The challenge we have today is people will discern and speak the heart of God, but then they add their own opinions, critical perceptions, personal judgments and then contend that this too is God. Such mixed discernment leads to condemnation and damnation rather than enlightenment, empowerment, and provoking Godly conviction and transformation and we know condemnation is not of God.

Romans 8:1-2 -There is therefore now no condemnation to them which are in Christ Jesus, who walk not after the flesh, but after the Spirit. For the law of the Spirit of life in Christ Jesus hath made me free from the law of sin and death.

The mixed discerner will share what God says then condemn with demeaning and religiously judgmental words or deeds that makes the person feel worthless, degraded, and despised by God; and even at times

38

damn the person to hell. This is not the heart of God but the heart of man and the devil. God is about life and empowerment and even when He is warning, judging, and expressing His anger, He is providing an opportunity for restoration and reconciliation.

John 10:10 - *The thief cometh not, but for to steal, and to kill, and to destroy: I am come that they might have life, and that they might have it more abundantly.*

John 3:17-18 - *For God sent not his Son into the world to condemn the world; but that the world through him might be saved. He that believeth on him is not condemned: but he that believeth not is condemned already, because he hath not believed in the name of the only begotten Son of God.*

Jesus was sent to save the world and for the purposes of us living and not dying, while living in abundance. The word *"believeth"* does not mean you say *"yes I believe in Jesus,"* and then live how you want. *"Believeth"* means a person is committed to and lives a lifestyle striving to demonstrate their belief. Jesus says those who do not believe are already condemned so there is no need for such a judgment. The judgment is automatic when we do not live in demonstration to our belief Him.

Many Christians have often defamed God, ruined their witness, and caused others to deny the discernment and will of God because of mixture. Many Christians will tell the truth then make an equally degrading comment to cause God's truth to be questioned. For example: *Homosexuality is not of God. I do not see how two people of the same sex could like one another anyway.* You discerned correctly then you killed it with a critical statement. It is the main reason the world is turning away from God, church, and God's way of living. Our words are not drawing people to God. Our words are solidifying the enemy's words in a person.

This is where the relationship with God and self-exploration is key to being a kingdom discerner. Relationship is where we receive the heart of God. It is also where He uses self-discernment to teach us what is of Him and what is not of Him. As we live in relationship with God, we learn how He behaves, responds, thinks, and feels. We acquire compassion as God shows us unconditional love despite our imperfections, and we in turn are able to display this same unconditional love to other people and situations.

Psalms 78:34-40 - When He slew [some of] them, [the remainder] inquired after Him diligently, and they repented and sincerely sought God [for a time]. And they [earnestly] remembered that God was their Rock, and the

Most High God their Redeemer. Nevertheless they flattered Him with their mouths and lied to Him with their tongues. For their hearts were not right or sincere with Him, neither were they faithful and steadfast to His covenant. But He, full of [merciful] compassion, forgave their iniquity and destroyed them not; yes, many a time He turned His anger away and did not stir up all His wrath and indignation. For He [earnestly] remembered that they were but flesh, a wind that goes and does not return. How often they defied and rebelled against Him in the wilderness and grieved Him in the desert!

Cultivating Kingdom Discernment in Your Life:

1. Ask God to use your life to develop your discernment.
2. Practice making your senses keen by implementing the following:
   - Spend time cultivating an open heaven over your life and home and ask God to use your discernment to show you the strongholds in your life, home, and community that need to be contended with to live under a consistent open heaven.
   - Spend time with the Holy Spirit discerning hidden strongholds, familiar spirits, and generational curses in your family line. Ask the Holy Spirit to teach you how to use the process of discernment, to judge the cultural and traditional behaviors, attitudes, and beliefs that are being passed down from generation to generation as good but may not be of God. As He helps you discern

41

these systems, spend time asking Him to
help you to discern the root so you can dig
these lies, evils, errors, and familiars
strongholds out of your family lineage.

Embodying Your Calling
As A Kingdom Watchman

We have different authorities and even
discern differently and uniquely depending
on our calling. Our judgments and ability
to operate in the spirit and natural realm
will be in alignment with the grace upon
our lives, as we accept and assert our ability
to glorify and operate in God through our
calling.

Luke 4:18

- The Spirit of the Lord is upon me
(God's authority and discernment is upon me)

- Because he hath anointed me to
preach the gospel to the poor (*Smell*)

- He hath sent me to heal the
brokenhearted (*Touch*)

- To preach deliverance to the
captives (*Hear*)

- And recovering of sight to the blind
(*Sight*)

- To set at liberty them that are
bruised (*Touch*)

Understanding our authority in relations to
our calling is essential to being unique and
not striving to operate as someone else.
Being oneself and understanding one's
place within the body is essential to
properly and keenly discerning, while being

able to SHIFT and transform lives, ministries, communities, atmospheres, and regions. Even God's plan for our lives has a specific authority and is strategically discerned.

Jeremiah 29:11 - *For I know (discern) the thoughts (authority) that I think toward you, saith the Lord, thoughts (authority) of peace (good), and not of evil (bad), to give you an expected end.*

God's Spirit upon us and heart within us, will manifest differently, but will bring about a prosperous and specifically designed end. Due to who we are as unique individuals, we will share the same standards and Godly truths, yet we will display a unique fashion of God, His authority, His discernment and His purpose for our existence.

Ephesians 4:11-16
And he gave some, apostles; and some, prophets; and some, evangelists; and some, pastors and teachers; For the perfecting of the saints, for the work of the ministry, for the edifying of the body of Christ: Till we all come in the unity of the faith, and of the knowledge of the Son of God, unto a perfect man, unto the measure of the stature of the fulness of Christ: That we henceforth be no more children, tossed to and fro, and carried about with every wind of doctrine, by the sleight of men, and cunning craftiness, whereby they lie in wait to deceive; But speaking

44

*the truth in love, may grow up into him in all
things, which is the head, even Christ: From
whom the whole body fitly joined together and
compacted by that which every joint supplieth,
according to the effectual working in the
measure of every part, maketh increase of the
body unto the edifying of itself in love.*

When Jesus gave us as gifts - apostles,
prophets, evangelists, pastors, teachers, He
bestowed an authority upon us for the
perfecting and equipping of the body of the
church. Jesus also gave us this authority so
we could discern and equip others to
discern between what was of Him and what
was not of Him. We were all given a
measure of authority so that the body of
Christ can increase through the
empowerment of love and unity.

• Effective kingdom watchman know their
  calling, accept their measure and
  understand that it is never less, but essential
  to advancing the kingdom.
• Effective kingdom watchmen equip
  themselves then seek to equip others in the
  fullness of God so they can discern between
  good and evil.
• Effective kingdom watchmen operate in
  love and unity.
• Effective kingdom watchmen empower
  others and seek to fitly join in the flow of
  what God is doing in the body of Christ and
  the world at large.

When discerning through the authority of your calling, you may sense through the following filters.

- *Apostles* sense atmospherically and how to bring the whole gospel and God's order to the particular people, church, ministry, body of Christ, community, region, nation, and the world
- *Prophets* sense futuristically - they sense through potential and possibilities.
- *Teachers* sense through empowerment and equipping - they sense through impartation, production and reproduction
- *Pastors* sense through concerns, emotions, compassion and the present state of a person, the church, a situation, and the world
- *Evangelists* sense through a need for reviving, salvation, renewal and restoration

Asserting Authority In Heavenly Realms
(Establishing position quickly & precisely in prayer)

The information in this chapter is in reference to entering into the heavenlies quickly and sustaining in your position so you will be able to progress successfully in warfare, intercession or in a service. This manner of prayer is different from just praying to God, as when we seek to open and maintain an open heaven, combat forces and establish God's kingdom, the enemy counterattacks. He is not willing to give up his territory, and will fight and use whatever legal ground available. The enemy will strive to thwart our prayers and take us out in the process.

One of the greatest keys to positioning ourselves in an authoritative stance that opens the heavenlies is to exalt God.

Exalt is *"rum"* in the Hebrew and means:
1. To rise, raise, bring up high
2. To be lifted up, extol, magnify

The enemy hates when we exalt God. God becomes so huge within the heavenlies, as we release adoration unto Him.

1Chronicles 16:28-29 - Give unto the Lord, ye kindreds of the people, give unto the Lord glory

47

and strength; Give unto the Lord the glory due unto his name: bring an offering, and come before him: worship the Lord in the beauty of holiness.

When we are giving unto the Lord glory and strength, exalting God in a bold, courageous vigor.

The Amplified Version - *Ascribe to the Lord, you families of the peoples, ascribe to the Lord glory and strength.*

Dictionary.com defines "*ascribe*" as:
1. To give credit or assign, as to a cause or source
2. Attribute; impute, assign to a source
3. Synonyms: accredit, attribute, charge, credit, hang on, lay, pin on, refer, reference

Dictionary.com defines a "*scribe*" as:
1. public clerk or writer,
2. an author, usually one having official status.

A scribe writes and when we write we make the vision plain - we establish it. When we exalt God, we are establishing His accreditation among the heavenlies and in and among the people and region. We are writing a decree that He is good and better than all who think they are Gods. Our words are being used to literally write in the atmosphere and upon the hearts of people

48

who God is, what His characteristics are....the quality of who He is as your God.

The Message Version of verse 28 reads -
Splendor and majesty flow out of him, strength and joy fill his place.

It is intriguingly interesting that we can give God strength. That we can release exaltation that makes Him even greater and powerful than what He already is. That's a level of glory and worship many of us haven't taped into yet. Our exaltation pushes/drives the devil out of our sphere while releasing the king of glory in our midst. This is a weapon the enemy cannot contend with. The enemy will therefore use an alternate means to find some legal ground to keep his position as the prince of the power of the air-the heavenlies and of this world *(Ephesians 2:2, 2Corinthians 4:4).*

Exaltation is about honor and the best way to release honor is through thanksgiving and praise. When we honor God, we access His gates and His courts. *Psalms 100:4* states that we are to "*Enter into his gates with thanksgiving, and into his courts with praise.*" There is no way to get anything out of a place without going through an entry point. Before you can access anything in a room, an office, a volt, the heavenlies, you must first enter in. Whether that be a door, window, gate; you have to enter in to access the goods.

49

When we come into the presence of one another, we must first enter in. Even on a phone or text, we have to go through a process to connect. We have to actually pick up the phone and dial or text the number. Even if we want something, the polite mannerism (honor) to initially display is to connect with a greeting before we further access our desires or needs.

Prayer is no different. God tells us to enter His gates with thanksgiving and His courts with praise. Gates are literal entry ways within the heavenlies that we go through to access God's kingdom. And courts are where His judgments take place.

The key of thanksgiving allows us to access beyond the gates. The key of praise grants us access into God's courts.

Even when Jesus taught the disciples how to pray, He revealed to them the importance of honor by exalting God.

Matthew 6:9 states - *After this manner therefore pray ye: Our Father which art in heaven, Hallowed be thy name.*

Dictionary.com defines "*hallowed*" as:
1. Regarded as holy; venerated; sacred
2. To make holy; sanctify; consecrate
3. To honor as holy; consider sacred; venerate

Hallowed exalts God as holy and sacred. It displays God's consecrated nature among all the heavenlies. We know where there is holiness, there is light and thus the glistening holiness of God dispels darkness. The word "Father" is a title of honor and with Jesus saying "Our Father" He specifically reveals who He is praying to. He is not praying to Buddha, Mary or any random idol God. He is specifically acknowledging His holy daddy who is in heaven. Though we do not have to use Jesus' exact words when praying, honor and acknowledgement of God alerts the heavenlies and the demonic realms of who is being glorified. Such exaltation positions us as the authoritarian in the spirit realm. By exalting God, we bypass any legal right for demonic forces to block our prayers.

The Message Version of that scripture states - *Our Father in heaven, Reveal who you are.*

This Message Version further confirms that as we exalt our daddy God, we are revealing His nature, character, power, sovereignty, matchlessness, HIS RULE OVER EVERYTHING & EVERYONE! Whewwwwww!

Jesus prayed further, "*Thy kingdom come. Thy will be done in earth, as it is in heaven (Matthew 6:10).*"

The Message Version declares - *Set the world right; Do what's best--as above, so below.*

Jesus is now positioned as the authoritarian among the heavenlies. By stating "thy kingdom come," he calls for a shifting in His sphere of influence so that His surroundings can take on the likeness of the kingdom of God. He is declaring the glory, nature, and character of God's presence to manifest.

One thing I learned about the glory is that it is already around us. The enemy is constantly at work so the spirit realm and the world tends to look like his kingdom. But God's glory is around us. When we are calling for the kingdom of God to come, we are not just activating and accessing glory from heaven, we are also revealing unconcealed glory that is hidden, lingering or neutralized within the earth and sphere around us.

Isaiah 63:7 states - *And one cried unto another, and said, Holy, holy, holy, is the LORD of hosts: the whole earth is full of his glory.*

As we call for the glory, God's presence fills up all around us and our sphere begins to feel and look like the kingdom of God. God begins to
"*set the world right*," such that His standard becomes our earthly and atmospheric standard.

Before conducting spiritual warfare or intercession, we should have already repented for our sins as continual daily repentance takes away the legal ground of the enemy and gives us pure authority to operate as ambassadors in the heavenlies. Sometimes, it is essential to repent again and to repent for the sins of those in our midst, as well as the sins of the region. It is also important to forgive and release forgiveness to debtors.

In Matthew 6:11, Jesus prays - *Give us this day our daily bread. And forgive us our debts, as we forgive our debtors.*

<u>*Debts* in the Greek is "*opheilema*" and means:</u>
1. That which is owed a debt metaph. dues: specifically of conjugal duty
2. Something owed, i. e. (figuratively) a due; morally, a fault: — debt
3. That which is owed that which is justly or legally due, a debt metaph. offence, sin

<u>*Debtors* in the Greek is "*opheiletes*" and means:</u>
1. An ower, i. e. person indebted; figuratively, a delinquent; morally, a transgressor (against God):— debtor, which owed, sinner.
2. One who owes another, a debtor one held by some obligation, bound by some duty

3. One who has not yet made amends to whom he has injured:

4. One who owes God penalty or whom God can demand punishment as something due, i. e. a sinner

This is where the enemy attempts to gain his legal ground. Though not always the case, this is also the reason we will enter the spirit realm or open up the heavenlies through praise and worship, but it is as if the glory of God does not abide among us. It will feel like the heavens have closed or our prayers are not penetrating. When this is happening, it is important to explore whether or not God was sufficiently honored such that we establish our authority in the heavenlies, or whether there is a debt that has not been repented of or forgiven. When God is honored the heavens will open and glory will be revealed. However, if repentance or forgiveness is an issue, the enemy will assume we owe him and he will fight us by overtaking the heavenlies and neutralizing the glory of God so that we think God is not among us or is not responding to our prayers. Repentance of our sins and forgiving our transgressors clears the debts by releasing the redemption of the work of the cross and God's unconditional love against the enemy.

When praying to open the heavenlies for a congregational service or for the purposes of warfare and intercession, repentance and forgiveness must advance to levels of repenting for the transgressions of the region, land, and groups of people as a whole.

2Chronicles 7:14 contends - *If my people, which are called by my name, shall humble themselves, and pray, and seek my face, and turn from their wicked ways; then will I hear from heaven, and will forgive their sin, and will heal their land.*

Generational and corporate repentance and forgiveness is necessary. This clears the legal rights of the enemy and enables the atmosphere or region to remain under God's rule and authority. The Holy Spirit will guide you in whether repentance and forgiveness is necessary and in what to repent. I will list some repentance considerations just to jolt your spirit in this area:

1. Repentance for sin within the church as a whole or even the body of Christ
2. Repentance for political decisions made in the community, region, or nation that are contrary to God's law or word
3. Repentance for murder, abortion and ungodly blood shed

4.   Repentance of sins done upon the land to which you are dwelling

5.   Repentance for sins of perversion, idolatry, witchcraft, and disobedience

6.   Sin against the house of God, gossip, betrayal, murmuring, and complaining

Jesus prays further in Matthew 5:13 - And lead us not into temptation, but deliver us from evil: For thine is the kingdom, and the power, and the glory, forever. Amen.

The Message Version - Keep us safe from ourselves and the Devil. You're in charge! You can do anything you want! You're ablaze in beauty! Yes. Yes. Yes.

Once we have repented and released forgiveness, deliverance evades which clears our debt and the debt of our debtors and solidifies our established position in the heavenlies. We have exalted God with praise and worship, called for a revealing and outpouring of God's glory, repented and released forgiveness where necessary. Now we are safely positioned to proceed into warfare, intercession and/or service plans, as we are now inside the gates and courts of God. We now have access to the kingdom of God and can further prevail against the enemy.

Open Heaven Decree

Lord we exalt you. We magnify you. We lift you up and declare that you are King of Kings! Lord of Lords! You are the only true and living God. We say expand yourself in our midst as we honor you. We say get huge! Get big! Be the limitless, enormous God that you are! You are so awesome to us. You are so powerful to us! You are so glorious to us! We can never get enough of praising you, worshipping you, glorifying you! We bow and surrender to forever edifying and magnifying you!

We bless you even now for being majestic. We bless you even now for being holy! We bless you even now for being precious, deaf defying, unexplainably exquisite. We bless you for being everything that we need and the world needs and declare that you reign, and your rule in us and among all the universe.

Lord we repent personally, ministerially, regionally, and generationally for every sin committed against you. We ask for your forgiveness and declare a blood washing of ourselves, the atmosphere, land, and region even now. We repent for everything that does not please or glorify you and receive a matchless blood washing by the redemptive blood of Jesus. We forgive all those who

have trespassed against us, while also
receiving forgiveness.

We declare a kingdom invasion through
your blood Jesus. And through your
grandiose power, we assert authority to
govern our earthly and heavenly sphere.
We command any blockages between you
and us to be thwarted and we declare we
live in open access to your covering and
your kingdom. Heaven is enmeshing with
our region even now and heaven is being
done in our midst even now. We call for
more of your glory to be revealed among us
and in us even now. We call for more of
your glory saturation and overtaking even
now. Holy Spirit let your four winds blow
in our midst as the arch angels come and
guard, war, and empower our midst even
now. We thank you God for the open
heavens and for reigning and ruling in our
sphere.

Governing God's Glory Realms!
Offensive In Warfare

A realm is a kingdom domain where a person or God asserts rulership, jurisdiction, and governmental authority.

As kingdom ambassadors of Jesus Christ, we have kingdom domain over the entire realm of earth and heaven.

Genesis 1:26-28 - And God said, Let us make man in our image, after our likeness: and let them have dominion over the fish of the sea, and over the fowl of the air, and over the cattle, and over all the earth, and over every creeping thing that creepeth upon the earth. So God created man in his own image, in the image of God created he him; male and female created he them. And God blessed them, and God said unto them, be fruitful, and multiply, and replenish the earth, and subdue it: and have dominion over the fish of the sea, and over the fowl of the air, and over every living thing that moveth upon the earth.

Ephesians 1:17-21 - That the God of our Lord Jesus Christ, the Father of glory, may give unto you the spirit of wisdom and revelation in the knowledge of him: The eyes of your understanding being enlightened; that ye may know what is the hope of his calling, and what the riches of the glory of his inheritance in the saints, And what is the exceeding greatness of his power to us- ward who believe, according to

*the working of his mighty power, Which he
wrought in Christ, when he raised him from the
dead, and set him at his own right hand in the
heavenly places, Far above all principality, and
power, and might, and dominion, and every
name that is named, not only in this world, but
also in that which is to come.*

***The Message Version** - That's why, when I
heard of the solid trust you have in the Master
Jesus and your outpouring of love to all the
Christians, I couldn't stop thanking God for
you--every time I prayed, I'd think of you and
give thanks. But I do more than thank. I ask--
ask the God of our Master, Jesus Christ, the God
of glory--to make you intelligent and discerning
in knowing him personally, your eyes focused
and clear, so that you can see exactly what it is
he is calling you to do, grasp the immensity of
this glorious way of life he has for Christians, oh,
the utter extravagance of his work in us who
trust him--endless energy, boundless strength!
All this energy issues from Christ: God raised
him from death and set him on a throne in deep
heaven, in charge of running the universe,
everything from galaxies to governments, no
name and no power exempt from his rule. And
not just for the time being, but forever.*

Jesus dying on the cross for our sins, then
rising in resurrection power over
everything, gave us the authority to rule
with Him over the heavens and the earth.

Ephesians 4:6- *And God raised us up with Christ and seated us with him in the heavenly realms in Christ Jesus.*

Romans 8:17 - *And if children, then heirs; heirs of God, and joint- heirs with Christ; if so be that we suffer with him, that we may be also glorified together.*

As we subdue and assert dominion, we are to:

• *Give God glory*
Psalms 29:2 - *Give unto the LORD the glory due unto his name; worship the LORD in the beauty of holiness.*

• *Establish ways for God to get glory*
Psalms 96:7-10 - *Give unto the Lord, O ye kindreds of the people, give unto the Lord the glory due unto his name: bring an offering, and come into his courts. O worship the Lord in the beauty of holiness: fear before him, all the earth. Say among the heathen that the Lord reigneth: the world also shall be established that it shall not be moved: he shall judge the people righteously.*

• *Experience the continual pleasures of God's glory*
Psalms 16:7 - *Thou wilt shew me the path of life: in thy presence is fulness of joy; at thy right hand there are pleasures for evermore.*

We accomplish this mandate by recognizing that God's glory is everywhere and is readily available to us as kingdom ambassadors.

Numbers 14:21 - But as truly as I live, all the earth shall be filled with the glory of the Lord.

Psalms 79:19 - And blessed be his glorious name for ever: and let the whole earth be filled with his glory; Amen, and Amen.

The Message Version - Blessed always his blazing glory! All earth brims with his glory.

Habakkuk 2:14 - For the earth shall be filled with the knowledge of the glory of the Lord, as the waters cover the sea.

God has filled the earth and the heavens with His glory so we will know that He created, owns and is in all things. He also wants us to recognize that He is always with us and is limitlessly assessable to us. Our spiritual and natural eyes have to be enlightened so we can recognize Him and receive the knowledge that nothing exists aside from Him.

2Corinthians 3:17-18 - Now the Lord is that Spirit: And where the Spirit of the Lord is, there is liberty. But we all, with open face beholding as in a glass the glory of the Lord, are changed into the same image from glory to glory, even as by the Spirit of the Lord.

The eyes of our understanding are enlightened when we pursue a relationship with God and live a lifestyle in Him (*with open face beholding as a glass-getting in God's face and letting Him change us*). We then go from glory to glory, being transfigured in Him, and being revealed His matchless glory. As we grow and SHIFT from glory to glory in God, we experience liberty in Him. His realms of glory that are all around us, become available to us. In order to assert authority over the glory realms we have achieved, we have to subdue and establish dominion. Otherwise they are available to us but can be overtaken at any time. This is because there is no proper acknowledgement that these realms have been accomplished, belong to someone, and are being governed by a particular kingdom. This is how Satan continues to have access and ascertain jurisdiction over areas of our natural lives and even the heavenlies that do not belong to him.

Matthew 16:19 - *And I will give unto thee the keys of the kingdom of heaven: and whatsoever thou shalt bind on earth shall be bound in heaven: and whatsoever thou shalt loose on earth shall be loosed in heaven.*

Whoever has the keys tends to have the power and the authority of a given place or thing. The key holder is also seen as the one who possesses the knowledge of who and

63

what goes in and out, and knowledge over what is being guarded and protected. If you have ever watched any of the *Chronicles of Narnia* movies, the key (knowledge) to the main actors' getting into other realms, was to actually go in the closet and access the realms. Once inside the closet, they transitioned into a new realm. They had the keys (knowledge) of the realm, and those in that realm recognized their power and authority simply by them being able to access it. However, this power and authority did not come by entering the realm. They had to continually visit the realm and learn how to live in that realm, gleam in that realm, and understand their authority and who they were in that realm, before they could actually govern it. If they would have just stayed on the outside of the closet or even just in the closet and never passed to the other side, they would have never realized the potential of what was available to them. They would have not become the kingdom kings and queens they were destined to be, would have never been able to save the people who were tied to their destiny, and they would have never been able to establish their rule and kingdom in that realm. This is the same with us. It is important that we reframe from just being free in Jesus, and elevating in Him, but then standing on the outside of the realms we have gained. We have to apply and further pursue the knowledge that comes with the keys we possess.

Though Satan is the prince of the powers of the air, we are kings and therefore have greater rulership. We have power over the fish of the sea, fowls of the air - including Satan and the airways, and every living thing upon the face of the earth.

Ephesians 2:2 - Wherein in time past ye walked according to the course of this world, according to the prince of the power of the air, the spirit that now worketh in the children of disobedience.

Genesis 1:26-28 - And God said, Let us make man in our image, after our likeness: and let them have dominion over the fish of the sea, and over the fowl of the air, and over the cattle, and over all the earth, and over every creeping thing that creepeth upon the earth. So God created man in his own image, in the image of God created he him; male and female created he them. And God blessed them, and God said unto them, be fruitful, and multiply, and replenish the earth, and subdue it: and have dominion over the fish of the sea, and over the fowl of the air, and over every living thing that moveth upon the earth.

God has given Satan permission to roam the earth, yet he owns nothing. Satan is already defeated and the only power he has is the power we give him through our sin and by not taking our rightful place as kingdom ambassadors.

1Peter 5:8 - *Be sober, be vigilant; because your adversary the devil, as a roaring lion, walketh about, seeking whom he may devour.*

Satan roams because he has no earthly home. He will remain restless until judgment day when he is cast into his eternal home of hell. We however, have been given total jurisdiction over the earth and the heavenlies as God mandated us as heirs to be *"fruitful, multiply, replenish, fill, subdue and have dominion."* We therefore determine how much authority we assert in the earth and heavenly realm.

Colossians 2:13-15 - *And you, being dead in your sins and the uncircumcision of your flesh, hath he quickened together with him, having forgiven you all trespasses; Blotting out the handwriting of ordinances that was against us, which was contrary to us, and took it out of the way, nailing it to his cross; And having spoiled principalities and powers, he made a shew of them openly, triumphing over them in it.*

<u>Spoil is "apekdyomai" in the Greek and means:</u>
1. to divest wholly oneself, or (for oneself) despoil
2. put off, spoil, wholly put off from one's self
3. denoting separation from what is put off
4. wholly to strip off for one's self (for one's own advantage) despoil, disarm

- When Jesus spoiled principalities He spoiled the rule and origin of the enemy.
- When Jesus spoiled powers He spoiled the authority, jurisdiction, strength, and liberty of the enemy.

Over is "*thriambeuo*" in the Greek and means:

1. to make an acclamatory procession,
2. i. e. (figuratively) to conquer or (by Hebraism) to give victory: — (cause)
3. to triumph (over), to have festival

Triumph in Webster's Dictionary means:

1. the act, fact, or condition of being victorious or triumphant; victory; conquest
2. a significant success or noteworthy achievement; instance or occasion of victory
3. exultation resulting from victory; joy over success
4. a public pageant, spectacle, or the like
5. to gain a victory; be victorious; win
6. to gain mastery; prevail: to triumph over fear
7. to be successful; achieve success
8. to exult over victory; rejoice over success
9. to be elated or glad; rejoice proudly; glory
10. to celebrate a triumph, experience extreme happiness
11. synonyms: celebration, elation, exultance, exultation, festivity, joy, jubilance, jubilation, jubilee, merriment, pride, rejoicing, reveling

Jesus triumphed over principalities and powers so that we could be restored in the authority God gave us before the fall of mankind. We are now SHIFTED to victors through Jesus Christ and can properly govern our realms of glory in heaven and in earth. It is time to daily give God glory, establish God's glory, and partake of God's glory realms.

The rest of this article was written by Nina Cook, my spiritual daughter.

To actually govern Gods realms you need to:
- Possess the key to those realms, and walk in the ability to use the key (welcome in and keep out)
- Have the mindset of the realm, holding its purposes, will, power and attributes
- Embody the realm, carry the realm in you, release the realms attributes around you
- Be in tuned with the realm, live in the realm constantly such that you can see, hear, and have all of your senses aligned with the realm and what is going on there
- Exercise the realm, experience and expose yourself to the realm often such that your exercise can be profitable to you and you can grow more keen, powerful, and authoritative within the realm

Jesus is our greatest example for overtaking realms. Jesus walked in both earthly and heavenly dominion simultaneously. Jesus ruled both and had the keys, so what happened in heaven, happened in earth as He commanded it forth. He was in tuned with God and heaven and sought to be like God and to please God.

John 5:19 - Then answered Jesus and said unto them, Verily, verily, I say unto you, The Son can do nothing of himself, but what he seeth the Father do: for what things soever he doeth, these also doeth the Son likewise.

John 5:30 - By myself I can do nothing; I judge only as I hear, and my judgment is just, for I seek not to please myself but him who sent me.

John 14:19 - Don't you believe that I am in the Father, and that the Father is in me? The words I say to you I do not speak on my own authority. Rather, it is the Father, living in me, who is doing his work.

Isaiah 22:22 - I will place on his shoulder the key to the house of David; what he opens no one can shut, and what he shuts no one can open.

Revelation 3:7 - And to the angel of the church in Philadelphia write; These things saith he that is holy, he that is true, he that hath the key of David, he that openeth, and no man shutteth; and shutteth, and no man openeth;

And we have this same power since we also have been given the keys and ability to rule in both.

John 14:12 - *Verily, verily, I say unto you, He that believeth on me, the works that I do shall he do also; and greater works than these shall he do; because I go unto my Father.*

Matthew 16:19 - *And I will give unto thee the keys of the kingdom of heaven: and whatsoever thou shalt bind on earth shall be bound in heaven: and whatsoever thou shalt loose on earth shall be loosed in heaven.*

Matthew 18:18 - *Truly I tell you, whatever you bind on earth will be bound in heaven, and whatever you loose on earth will be loosed in heaven.*

Jesus is the key holder, and we are joint heirs with Christ through His resurrection and are now also key holders. So whatever we bind, declare, and loose on earth as Kings and possessors of the land it shall be bound, declared and loosed in heaven also as we are Kings in heaven as well.

We have to walk in this level of knowledge of our authority in order to govern the realms. We are key holders which means that we have unlimited entrance and exit in and out of the realms, we can open and shut the doors. We can authorize what we want to come in and out of the earth.

We have to have the understanding that we operate both on earth and in heavenly realms, such that we can possess it, dominate it, and then embody the mindset of that realm. Jesus embodied the mindset of heaven. Jesus knew who He was at all times, He knew His purpose, and knew the power, dominion, and authority that He possessed when He came down from heaven. This is a good example and model for us because although we are seated in heavenly places, we too are walking the earth. When Jesus came down He still knew that He had the keys to the kingdom and to all realms. He embodied the realm of heaven when He came down, and although His natural body was not directly in the realm but here on earth, He still carried and dominated it. We must do the same.

John 6:38- For I have come down from heaven, not to do my own will but the will of him who sent me.

We discern from this scripture that Jesus had the mindset of the realm in which He governed. The mindset was to do His Fathers will. He came down from heaven but did not discard of it. A key in us being able to successfully govern realms is to always possess the knowledge, will, and purposes of the realm and to embody it, demonstrate it, and release it.

John 5:19 - *Then answered Jesus and said unto them, Verily, verily, I say unto you, The Son can do nothing of himself, but what he seeth the Father do: for what things soever he doeth, these also doeth the Son likewise.*

Jesus was so in tune and aligned with the realm of heaven that He was able to steadily look into the realm, and His eyes saw each step that He was to take here on earth. He lived in the realm of heaven and consistently had His eyes and senses open to the knowledge, will, and purposes within the realm.

<u>*Seeth* in the Hebrew is *"blepo"* and means:</u>

1. to see, discern, of the bodily eye with the bodily eye
2. to be possessed of sight, have the power of seeing perceive by the use of the eyes
3. look descry to turn the eyes to anything
4. to look at, look upon, gaze at to perceive by the senses
5. to feel to discover by use, to know by experience.

Jesus looked, gazed upon, discerned, and perceived the will of the Father at all times. One of the Hebrew definitions of **seeth** is *"to feel to discover by use, and to know by experience."* Jesus knew by experience and by use. This is key to governing Gods glory realms. It is only by exercise and experience within these realms that you will be able to

72

successfully govern your realms and then go from realm to realm.

1 Timothy 4:8 - *For bodily exercise profiteth little: but godliness is profitable unto all things, having promise of the life that now is, and of that which is to come.*

The Amplified Bible - *For physical training is of some value (useful for a little), but godliness (spiritual training) is useful and of value in everything and in every way, for it holds promise for the present life and also for the life which is to come.*

Spiritual exercise and training is profitable and useful in everything and in every way. And it holds promise of the life that now is and that which is to come. Living a lifestyle of pursing the overtaking realms allows us to walk in the blessing, and fulfillment that is available to us in this present life. Exercising, exploring, and having experience within the realms will bring growth, transformation and knowledge to you through the training and exposure that you receive. Thus your ability to govern will constantly be improved where you will look just like your Father in Heaven. Doing what God does which is to rule and reveal and fill the earth and the heavens with glory.

Glory Realm Activation:

1. Ask God to show you His glory in everything and every person you encounter as you go throughout the day.

2. As God reveals Himself to you, praise and worship Him for what He shows you and even share what you are seeing with others so that God can get greater glory.

3. Ask God to show you places, situations, things and people throughout the day that do not possess His glory. If God leads you, assert authority over those places, things, and people and declare that His glory is being revealed and established in that place, thing, situation or person.

4. Ask God to open up His heavenly realms to you and show you your purpose and how to properly govern in your heavenly realms.

5. Ask Him to teach you how to operate in these realms so that you can cleanse out principalities and powers that may have taken up residence in your sphere. Ask Him to teach you how to open up the heavens and establish His heavenly principalities and glory in those realms.

Glory Realm Decree

We decree realms of your glory God! We ask for your royal domain to be opened up to us - let your kingdom invade with power. We decree realms of your glory in our region, in our sphere, in our domain. We decree heaven is prevailing even now, we decree your glory is dominating even now.

We decree limitless realms are our portion. We decree realms are opening up for visions, and we are having visions of seeing you, and experiencing heaven, seeing the potential and fruit of heaven, we declare that it is accessible and tangible in the earth, and we are able to release it in the earth. We declare we are receiving words of knowledge, prophecy, wisdom, understanding, counsel, answers, and strategies even now. We are hearing and seeing you clearly and we are being consumed in what you are speaking and saying to us, it is becoming us. We're changing because of what you are speaking and showing Lord. As we soak in your glory we soak up your word, we soak up your essence. We thank you that your providence and your field is our realm and we say more.

Even as your realms are among us we say your waves of glory are overtaking us even now. We are experiencing your waves billowing us, saturating us, flooding us. We

are being gushed by your waves, we are
being transposed by your waves. They are
rippling and cleaving to us. We are
changing in your waves, we are becoming
personal in your waves. We are not just
encountering your presence we are being
transformed, made anew, and revived.

We seek change into your character and in
your nature. We expect it to manifest! More
Jesus! More Jesus. More uprising and
solidifying of our identity and dominion
Jesus. More dismantling demonic forces in
and among us Jesus. More making us
abandoned worshippers and kingdom
ambassadors Jesus. More stirring in us
Jesus unto obedience to your will and ways
for our lives. More working miracles in us
and through us Jesus! More embellishment
in your waves of glory for we resemble and
correctly represent you Jesus. Let
wholeness take over us as we embrace and
subdue realms of your glory.

Flowing In & With The Holy Spirit

The most important strategy for making sure prayers penetrate and accomplish their required task is flowing in and with the Holy Spirit as one unit - one army. In order to flow as one unit, there must be agreement.

Amos 3:3 - *Can two walk together, except they be agreed?*

The Message Version - *Do two people walk hand in hand if they aren't going to the same place?*

The word walk is "*yalak*" in the Greek and means:
1.   to flow, to carry, to march,
2.   to go, walk, come, depart, proceed, move, go away
3.   prosper, pursue, cause to run, spread, take away ((- journey))

When we are praying as a group or ministry, there should be a flow of agreement. We should all have the same goal, prayer assignment, and should be able to flow as one unit to efficiently accomplish our prayer task.

Even when the people were waiting to receive the Holy Spirit on the day of Pentecost, they were all on one accord.

Acts 2:1-2 - And when the day of Pentecost was fully come, they were all with one accord in one place. And suddenly there came a sound from heaven as of a rushing mighty wind, and it filled all the house where they were sitting. And there appeared unto them cloven tongues like as of fire, and it sat upon each of them. And they were all filled with the Holy Ghost, and began to speak with other tongues, as the Spirit gave them utterance.

<u>*Accord* is "*homothymadon*" in the Greek and means:</u>

1. unanimously, with one accord (mind).
2. with one mind, with one accord, with one passion-
3. a unique Greek word, used 10 of its 12 New Testament occurrences in the Book of Acts, helps us understand the uniqueness of the Christian community. *Homothumadon* is a compound of two words meaning *"to rush along"* and *"in unison."* The image is almost musical; a number of notes are sounded, which while different, harmonize in pitch and tone. As the instruments of a great concert under the direction of a concert master, so the Holy Spirit blends together the lives of members of Christ's church.

Homonthumadon, which is the Greek word for *"accord"* contends that being in unison is almost musical. It is like singing a beautiful harmonious song together. The definition contends that even though there are different sounds (different people, personalities & gifts, different types of prayer styles), all are harmonious in pitch and tone (one passion).

- **Pitch** denotes the degree of height or depth of a tone or of sound
- **Tone** denotes quality or character of sound.

The people were on one accord as they were waiting to receive the Holy Spirit. They were hanging out together in expectation to receive what Jesus had promised. They were most likely thinking and talking on the things of God and what was to come, maybe praising and worshipping, possibly searching scriptures - or maybe just fellowshipping. But they were united with expectation to receive the Holy Spirit. They were also in one place - postured together - positioned together in the same atmosphere, while displaying the same passion and desire - the same pitch and tone - the same sound. This yields revelation that when we as a prayer ministry desire to receive something from God, we must position ourselves in expectation. Our position must be in the same realm - the same passion. One person cannot be praying from earth while the other is in heaven. One person cannot be in the second heaven combating demons, while the other is thinking about laundry or wishing they were taking a nap, and another is in the throne room with God. One person cannot have the mindset that the prayer assignment is stupid or worthless, while another cannot wait to beat the devil down. Every person must have the same expectation, perspective and passion for the task at hand.

In addition, being on one accord helps determine the sound/position that we pray from. There is a frequency (sound) for every position of prayer and if we are on different wave links then we are producing multiple sounds instead of one, which is really chaotic and hinders the full manifestation of what God may want to do in our midst. This could also cause the prayer ministry to miss God's sound (tone, pitch, frequency) because the sound we are listening for and releasing is not the sound that God is producing.

The scripture says that as they were all on one accord, and *suddenly there came a sound from heaven as of a rushing mighty wind.* That sound as a mighty rushing wind was the Holy Spirit. It was as if God responded with the same or even greater intense urgency and passion (pitch and tone) to which they did as they postured in expectation to receive the Holy Spirit. Their unity caused the Holy Spirit to fill the house, while sitting upon each person like cloven fire. WHEWWWW! The Holy Spirit filled the atmosphere while personally encountering every person with the burning presence of God. WHEWWWW!

Cloven in dictionary.com is defined as:

1. a past particle of cleave and cleave means to adhere closely, stick, cling, to remain faithful

2. Synonyms are open, rend, split, pierce, separate

When the cloven fire came and sat upon the 120, they all became filled with the Holy Spirit. The cloven fire opened, split, and pierced each of them such that the Holy Spirit could then enter them and stick, cling, adhere closely, and then remain faithful within them. God said He would never leave nor forsake us (*Hebrews 13:5, Deuteronomy 31:6*). He was activating and solidifying His word in them.

As each person encountered the Holy Spirit, they were filled with the Holy Spirit and began to speak in tongues as the Spirit gave them utterance. I would say that they each where filled with the Holy Spirit and began to speak mysteries, prophecies, words of knowledge, as the Holy Spirit gave them utterances. I state this because though we may not know at times what we are saying when we speak in tongues, we are speaking an actual language. We are either edifying others, ourselves, or the world around us. Thus we are releasing the word, heart, authority and will of God into ourselves, people, the atmosphere, and region (1Corinthians 12, 1Corinthians 14). The Holy Spirit lives in us to guide, comfort, teach and empower us to know Jesus, live for Him and to do His will. The 120 were releasing revelation, prophecy etc., into the atmosphere as the Holy Spirit led and revealed Himself unto them.

John 14:26 - But the Comforter, which is the Holy Ghost, whom the Father will send in my name, he shall teach you all things, and bring all things to your remembrance, whatsoever I have said unto you.

John 15:26 - When the Advocate comes, whom I will send to you from the Father--the Spirit of truth who goes out from the Father--he will testify about me.

This revelation is important in prayer ministry because as we are on one accord, it allows us to align quickly with heaven so that God's presence can fill our atmosphere, while the Holy Spirit overtakes us. As the Holy Spirit empowers each prayer warrior, he or she is able to provide further revelation to assist with the prayer assignment. When we are praying for an assignment, the only way we should be without direction, answers, tools, and strategies is if God is designing it that way. And even then we should have a knowing that it is Him orchestrating the prayer in that manner. Otherwise, we should be acquiring prophecies, revelation, words of knowledge, interpretation, and wisdom, as each person is empowered by the Holy Spirit.

Mark 4:11 - And he said unto them, unto you it is given to know the mystery of the kingdom of God: but unto them that are without, all these things are done in parables:

John 16:13 - Howbeit when he, the Spirit of truth, is come, he will guide you into all truth: for he shall not speak of himself; but whatsoever he shall hear, that shall he speak: and he will shew you things to come.

Romans 8:26 - Likewise the Spirit also helpeth our infirmities: for we know not what we should pray for as we ought: but the Spirit itself maketh intercession for us with groanings which cannot be uttered.

Isaiah 11:2 - The Spirit of the LORD will rest on him-- the Spirit of wisdom and of understanding, the Spirit of counsel and of might, the Spirit of the knowledge and fear of the LORD.

1Corinthians 2:13 - And we impart this in words not taught by human wisdom but taught by the Spirit, interpreting spiritual truths to those who are spiritual.

1John 2:20 - But ye have an unction from the Holy One, and ye know all things.

Agreement - walking in unity - or in this case flowing in and with the spirit signifies covenant. In marriage, a threefold cord is a covenant between God, husband and wife.

Ecclesiastes 4:12 - And if one prevail against him, two shall withstand him; and a threefold cord is not quickly broken.

In prayer, the threefold cord is a covenant between the Holy Spirit, the prayer team, and the prayer assignment. We see in this scripture the power of the threefold cord. One covenant partner can be defeated. Two can barely overcome. If either is out of agreement, it hinders the effectiveness of the prayer, and the ability for the prayer to accomplish its tasks. But if everyone is in agreement, breakthrough manifests.

We also see here that in order to flow effectively, the Holy Spirit has to be the head and then we come into alignment with what He is speaking and leading us to do regarding the prayer assignment. It is no different than the husband and wife in marriage. God aligns the husband and the husband aligns the wife and family. The Holy Spirit aligns us, and then we align the prayer assignment, the people we are praying for, the ministry, and the region.

Because we are aligned with the Holy Spirit, our prayers should flow one to another and should be synchronized with one another. As each prayer warrior prays, he or she should further penetrate what has already been prayed, or add to what has already been prayed.

1Corinthians 13:9 - *For we know in part, and we prophesy in part.*

Exodus 23:30 - *By little and little I will drive them out from before thee, until thou be increased, and inherit the land.*

1 Corinthians 12:6-20 - *Now there are diversities of gifts, but the same Spirit. And there are differences of administrations, but the same Lord. And there are diversities of operations, but it is the same God which worketh all in all. But the manifestation of the Spirit is given to every man to profit withal. For to one is given by the Spirit the word of wisdom; to another the word of knowledge by the same Spirit; To another faith by the same Spirit; to another the gifts of healing by the same Spirit; To another the working of miracles; to another prophecy; to another discerning of spirits; to another divers kinds of tongues; to another the interpretation of tongues: But all these worketh that one and the selfsame Spirit, dividing to every man severally as he will.*

For as the body is one, and hath many members, and all the members of that one body, being

85

many, are one body: so also is Christ. For by one Spirit are we all baptized into one body, whether we be Jews or Gentiles, whether we be bond or free; and have been all made to drink into one Spirit.-- For the body is not one member, but many. If the foot shall say, because I am not the hand, I am not of the body; is it therefore not of the body? And if the ear shall say, because I am not the eye, I am not of the body; is it therefore not of the body? If the whole body were an eye, where were the hearing? If the whole were hearing, where were the smelling? But now hath God set the members every one of them in the body, as it hath pleased him. And if they were all one member, where were the body?

But now are they many members, yet but one body. And the eye cannot say unto the hand, I have no need of thee: nor again the head to the feet, I have no need of you. Nay, much more those members of the body, which seem to be more feeble, are necessary:

As we flow together and build upon one another's prayer, initially, it is important to know what one another's gifts and strengths are, esteem one another, and provide avenues for everyone to be used and to grow.

1Corinthians 10:5-10 *- Who then is Paul, and who is Apollos, but ministers by whom ye believed, even as the Lord gave to every man? I have planted, Apollos watered; but God gave the increase. So then neither is he that planteth any* *thing, neither he that watereth; but God that giveth the increase. Now he that planteth and he that watereth are one: and every man shall receive his own reward according to his own labour.*

For we are labourers together with God: ye are God's husbandry, ye are God's building. According to the grace of God which is given unto me, as a wise masterbuilder, I have laid the foundation, and another buildeth thereon. But let every man take heed how he buildeth thereupon.

Paul clearly knew his gifts and calling and He knew Apollos' gifts and calling. They were not in competition with one another as Paul makes it clear that both were needed for the building of the kingdom of God. It is God that answers our prayers (bring the increase) and it is God who rewards us for our ministry endeavors. This is key in prayer ministry because it will take hard work and self-sacrifice to truly submit to the ministry. If your mindset is about what you can get, and feeling someone owes you something because of the time and investment you give to the ministry, then your focus is off and is in disagreement with the covenant. Such disagreement hinders the flow of the Holy Spirit and the ability to get prayers answered. God rewards those who diligently seek and work for Him.

Hebrews 11:6 - *But without faith it is impossible to please him: for he that cometh to God must believe that he is, and that he is a rewarder of them that diligently seek him.*

I believe it is okay to say to God that you are feeling weary and a bit underappreciated, and would like Him to bless you or even show you where He has blessed you for your ministry endeavors. It is religious to assume that God is so selfish and self-absorbed that He wants us to pour out in ministry and never expect Him to reward us. The bible states the following:

Proverbs 11:25 - *The liberal soul shall be made fat: and he that watereth shall be watered also himself.*

Matthew 7:11 - *ye then, being evil, know how to give good gifts unto your children, how much more shall your Father which is in heaven give good things to them that ask him?*

Psalms 84:11 - *For the LORD God is a sun and shield; the LORD bestows favor and honor; no good thing does he withhold from those whose walk is blameless.*

Romans 8:32 - *He who did not spare his own Son, but gave him up for us all--how will he not also, along with him, graciously give us all things?*

Matthew 7:7-8 - Ask, and it shall be given you; seek, and ye shall find; knock, and it shall be opened unto you: For everyone who asks receives; the one who seeks finds; and to the one who knocks, the door will be opened.

In saying this, God is the one who rewards and increases. Therefore, it is important to maintain a posture of servant hood and seek God, not your leader, not the church, but God, for rewards. God gives the best gifts and will bless you like no one else ever could.

Ephesians 3:20 - Now unto him that is able to do exceeding abundantly above all that we ask or think, according to the power that worketh in us.

Likewise, it is also important for leaders to have balance and to let people know they are appreciated and that you recognize who they are in God and all they do for His kingdom. It is innate for people to want to be esteemed and empowered. The whole reason why we worship God is to tell Him how good He is and how much we appreciate Him. We are made in His likeness and therefore, we have an innate need to be encouraged in our identity and worth.

Philippians 2:3 - Let nothing be done through strife or vainglory; but in lowliness of mind let each esteem other better than themselves.

Romans 12:10 - *Be devoted to one another in love. Honor one another above yourselves.*

1Peter 3:8 - *Finally, all of you, be like-minded, be sympathetic, love one another, be compassionate and humble.*

Cultivating a prayer ministry of empowering one another in who each prayer warrior is and in their giftings and callings, allows for a greater manifestation of the power of the Holy Spirit to operate and flow, while experiencing the *Pentecost suddenly* of heaven responding to and answering your prayers.

The word of God contends that we should receive power once we receive the Holy Spirit.

Acts 1:8 - *But ye shall receive power, after that the Holy Ghost is come upon you: and ye shall be witnesses unto me both in Jerusalem, and in all Judaea, and in Samaria, and unto the uttermost part of the earth.*

Romans 15:13 - *May the God of hope fill you with all joy and peace in believing, so that by the power of the Holy Spirit you may abound in hope.*

In being filled with the Holy Spirit, the power of God should be evident in our lives. As we are filled, we should flow with power and expect to be powerful in God.

Ephesians 6-10 - *Finally, my brethren, be strong in the Lord, and in the power of his might.*

Romans 15:13 - *May the God of hope fill you with all joy and peace in believing, so that by the power of the Holy Spirit you may abound in hope.*

Luke 4:24 - *And, behold, I send the promise of my Father upon you: but tarry ye in the city of Jerusalem, until ye be endued with power from on high.*

In *Luke 4:24*, Jesus tells the disciples to wait in Jerusalem and expect to be endued with power from on high. That word *"endued"* means *"to be clothed or arrayed."* Basically they were expecting to be clothed, like a garment or uniform, in the power of the Holy Spirit. During my personal prayer time, I consistently ask the Holy Spirit to soak me in His tangible power and might. I just rest (tarry) in His presence as He absorbs and endows me with power. As prayer warriors and Spirit filled saints, we should be consumed by and operating in the tangible power of God. Pursue Holy Spirit's power and expect miracles, signs and wonders to flow through you.

Acts 4:31 - And when they had prayed, the place was shaken where they were assembled together; and they were all filled with the Holy Ghost, and they spake the word of God with boldness.

It is essential to rely on the Holy Spirit as you pray. Do not be repetitious or try to pray like someone else. Be yourself and let God use you through the anointing that is on your life. As each prayer warrior and the prayer ministry as a whole grows, you will partake of one another's giftings and anointings. Sometimes you will sound like another person or flow in a gift that you normally do not operate in. This is because the Holy Spirit has no measure or limits. The more you are open to being used, the more He will use you for God's glory.

Matthew 6:7 - But when ye pray, use not vain repetitions, as the heathen [do]: for they think that they shall be heard for their much speaking. **Attempting to pray repetitious or like someone else, causes you to covet and operate in false pride that is really insecurity.**

Luke 4:18 - The Spirit of the Lord [is] upon me, because he hath anointed me to preach the gospel to the poor; he hath sent me to heal the brokenhearted, to preach deliverance to the captives, and recovering of sight to the blind, to set at liberty them that are bruised. **Praying through your own anointing allows you to**

92

operate in the mantle and mandate of God that is on your life.

It is okay to use prayer books, written decrees and other prayer material as the Holy Spirit leads. Make sure the Holy Spirit is guiding you as books and the like are strategies and weapons. You want to make sure you are using the correct strategy and weapon for the prayer assignment at hand and not just implementing something that sounded great in a book.

When preparing for a prayer meeting, seek the Holy Spirit for the following:

• What is the purpose and desired outcome of the assignment?
• Are you praying for people, the ministry, region, or all the above?
• What warfare are you to complete? What demons, strongholds, principalities, and powers, are you to combat?
• What are the strategies and weapons for warfare and completing the assignment?
• The prayer flow: Holy Spirit may or may not give you a prayer flow as He may wait until you are all together. But in asking, explore the following:

A. How should you start and proceed: Should you start in worship, warfare, repentance, tongues, marching, etc.

B. Who should pray first, second, etc. (Julie, then John, then Jacob)

- Pray into what the Holy Spirit gives you, as sometimes He will have you complete what He gives you beforehand and release an entire different strategy when the prayer ministry meets.

Discerning People, Devils, Atmospheres & Heavenly Realms

Discerning people, devils, atmospheres and heavens around us is essential to recognizing whether the place we are in is already dedicated to God or requires dedication to God.

Genesis 28:10-18

And Jacob went out from Beersheba, and went toward Haran. And he lighted upon a certain place, and tarried there all night, because the sun was set; and he took of the stones of that place, and put them for his pillows, and lay down in that place to sleep. And he dreamed, and behold a ladder set up on the earth, and the top of it reached to heaven: and behold the angels of God ascending and descending on it. And, behold, the Lord stood above it, and said, I am the Lord God of Abraham thy father, and the God of Isaac: the land whereon thou liest, to thee will I give it, and to thy seed; And thy seed shall be as the dust of the earth, and thou shalt spread abroad to the west, and to the east, and to the north, and to the south: and in thee and in thy seed shall all the families of the earth be blessed.

And, behold, I am with thee, and will keep thee in all places whither thou goest, and will bring thee again into this land; for I will not leave thee, until I have done that which I have spoken to thee of. And Jacob awaked out of his sleep, and he said, Surely the Lord is in this place; and I knew it not. And he was afraid, and said, How dreadful is this place! This is none other but the house of God, and this is the gate of heaven. And Jacob rose up early in the morning, and took the stone that he had put for his pillows, and set it up for a pillar, and poured oil upon the top of it. And he called the name of that place Bethel: but the name of that city was called Luz at the first.

Before Jacob went to sleep, he did not discern the atmosphere and the heavens around him. He had been journeying a while, and since the sun had set, he retreated into a place he felt was safe for the night. Jacob prepared the place so he could rest as he took stones for pillows and went to sleep. As Jacob slept, he appeared to have a powerful prophetic dream. Jacob woke up and said *"Surely the Lord is in this place; and I knew it not."* Jacob recognized that he was not just dreaming but was having a divine visitation from the Lord. The heavens and revelation was available to him even before he went to sleep, but he did not discern his surroundings or meditate upon the Lord. All throughout the bible, scripture encourages us to mediate upon God day and night. Early morning and night meditation is essential to discerning God's presence and opening gateways, and receiving strategies and prophetic downloads. We are in a quiet place of rest so God tends to speak and share things that we may not be postured to hear during the day.

Psalms 4:4-5 - Stand in awe, and sin not: commune with your own heart upon your bed, and be still. Selah. Offer the sacrifices of righteousness, and put your trust in the Lord.

Joshua 1:6 - This book of the law shall not depart out of thy mouth; but thou shalt meditate therein day and night, that thou mayest observe to do according to all that is written therein: for then thou shalt make thy way prosperous, and then thou shalt have good success.

Psalms 63:5-6 - My soul shall be satisfied as with marrow and fatness; and my mouth shall praise thee with joyful lips: When I remember thee upon my bed, and meditate on thee in the night watches.

Psalms 119:147-148 - I was up before sunrise, crying for help, hoping for a word from you. I stayed awake all night, prayerfully pondering your promise.

Psalm 119:55 - In the night, LORD, I remember your name, that I may keep your law.

Psalm 119:148 - My eyes stay open through the watches of the night, that I may meditate on your promises.

Psalms 1:2 - But whose delight is in the law of the LORD, and who meditates on his law day and night.

As Jacob woke from sleep, he said, "*How dreadful is this place! This is none other but the house of God, and this is the gate of heaven.*" The word *dreadful* means "*feared or referenced*" in the Hebrew. Jacob was now discerning that he was in an atmosphere of God and had slept under an open heaven, which provided a gateway to heaven and to God.

When I lay down to sleep, I will spend time communing with God. I will use the blood of Jesus and fire of God to cleanse myself from sin and daily challenges, worship God and just soak myself in His presence. This SHIFTS me to resting in His secret place. If God wants to share something with me or wants me to remain awake to talk or pray, I am able to easily discern that. I am also able to better discern when I am encountering Him at night, and He will let me know if I am to remain sleep as He communes with me or if I am to awaken to journal, intercede, war, worship.

Jacob was challenged that he did not discern that the place he was in was cultivated with the presence of God and possessed an open heaven. To make sure no one else made the same mistake of entering the Lord's presence and not recognizing it, Jacob set pillows as a monument, anointed them, and changed the name of the place to "*Bethel.*" *Bethel* in the Hebrew means "*the house of God.*"

Even though Jacob was sleep, His Spirit was still sharpened enough to discern and receive the word and plan of God through a prophetic dream. This is because God is a Spirit and He never sleeps or slumber *(Psalms 121:1-5....Behold, he that keepeth Israel shall neither slumber nor sleep)*. And though we sleep, our Spirit should always be postured to discern the atmosphere around us and to commune with Him.

Matthew 26:35-41
Then cometh Jesus with them unto a place called Gethsemane, and saith unto the disciples, Sit ye here, while I go and pray yonder. And he took with him Peter and the two sons of Zebedee, and began to be sorrowful and very heavy. Then saith he unto them, my soul is exceeding sorrowful, even unto death: tarry ye here, and watch with me.

And he went a little further, and fell on his face, and prayed, saying, O my Father, if it be possible, let this cup pass from me: nevertheless not as I will, but as thou wilt. And he cometh unto the disciples, and findeth them asleep, and saith unto Peter, What, could ye not watch with me one hour? Watch and pray, that ye enter not into temptation: the spirit indeed is willing, but the flesh is weak.

Jesus told the disciples that their Spirit was willing but their flesh was weak. The disciples' flesh was not submitted enough to their Spirit to remain awake and alert. They were not only naturally falling asleep but were asleep spiritually. Their Spirit knew what was at hand, however, their flesh dominated their Spirit, and caused them not to truly discern the times, seasons, and danger of Jesus' fate. They were dull to sensing the urgency of prophecy being fulfilled, and the necessity of preparing themselves to deal with Jesus being put into captivity and ultimately dying on the cross. Had the disciples been spiritually awake, they would have been able to subject their flesh to remaining awake and being on guard and praying as God had required. As a result of weak flesh, the disciples made some bad decisions leading into the crucifixion of Jesus *(cutting off ears, denying Jesus, panicking, not believing he rose).* Had the disciples been spiritually awake and alert, they might have handled the situation better though they could not prevent it.

Acts 2 is a prime example of the importance of discerning people, atmospheres, and regions correctly.

When the 120 received the Holy Spirit on the day of Pentecost, many perceived them to be drunk and even mocked them

Acts 2:12-13 *- And they were all amazed, and were in doubt, saying one to another, What meaneth this? Others mocking said, these men are full of new wine.*

100

They failed to discern the strong presence of God speaking through the people, in the atmosphere and even did not recognize that prophecy was being fulfilled among them.

Verse 14-17 - But Peter, standing up with the eleven, lifted up his voice, and said unto them, Ye men of Judaea, and all ye that dwell at Jerusalem, be this known unto you, and hearken to my words: For these are not drunken, as ye suppose, seeing it is but the third hour of the day. But this is that which was spoken by the prophet Joel; And it shall come to pass in the last days, saith God, I will pour out of my Spirit upon all flesh: and your sons and your daughters shall prophesy, and your young men shall see visions, and your old men shall dream dreams.

A regional work was being done with unifying people through a supernatural power of God's presence.

Verse 7-11 - Now when this was noised abroad, the multitude came together, and were confounded, because that every man heard them speak in his own language. And they were all amazed and marvelled, saying one to another, Behold, are not all these which speak Galilaeans? And how hear we every man in our own tongue, wherein we were born? Parthians, and Medes, and Elamites, and the dwellers in Mesopotamia, and in Judaea, and Cappadocia, in Pontus, and Asia, Phrygia, and Pamphylia, in Egypt, and in

101

the parts of Libya about Cyrene, and strangers of Rome, Jews and proselytes, Cretes and Arabians, we do hear them speak in our tongues the wonderful works of God.

It was not until they were reminded of the prophecy and the power of Jesus that they believed and desired to receive.

Verse 37-38 - *Now when they heard this, they were pricked in their heart, and said unto Peter and to the rest of the apostles, Men and brethren, what shall we do? Then Peter said unto them, Repent, and be baptized every one of you in the name of Jesus Christ for the remission of sins, and ye shall receive the gift of the Holy Ghost.*

God says He will use the foolish things to confound the wise.

1Corinthians 1-27-28 - *For ye see your calling, brethren, how that not many wise men after the flesh, not many mighty, not many noble, are called: But God hath chosen the foolish things of the world to confound the wise; and God hath chosen the weak things of the world to confound the things which are mighty; And base things of the world, and things which are despised, hath God chosen, yea, and things which are not, to bring to nought things that are.*

When we enter a place, we must use spiritual discernment to judge what is of God and what is not of Him. Practice by consistently asking the Holy Spirit to teach you discernment when you are among family members, friends, in stores, at church, on the job, in the community, in different cities, states, and nations.

When spiritually discerning implement the following:

- Discern the people (what are they doing, saying, does it agree with the Spirit of God in you or line up with the bible)
- Search for the presence of God (is the Holy Spirit among you or is evil, mixture, a form of godliness among you) 2 *Timothy 3:5 - Having a form of godliness, but denying the power thereof: from such turn away*).
- Explore if any prophecies, words of knowledge, promises are being fulfilled or established.
- Ask God what is He desiring or doing in the atmosphere and even in the region and discern accordingly.
- If God's presence and will is not operating, ask Him for a strategy in SHIFTING the atmosphere. Be open to what God says as He may lead you to complete the following:
- Take authority over the atmosphere through prayer, declaration, exaltation of Him
- Dismantle demonic forces as the Holy Spirit leads
- Utilization of spiritual weapons (clapping, shouting, praising dancing,

marching, declaring the word, applying the blood of Jesus, etc.)

- Prophecy, exhort, release a word of knowledge, wisdom, understanding, counsel to a person, to people as a whole, or into the atmosphere as true SHIFTERS can change the atmosphere by just walking in the room. You do not always have to be on the microphone or in direct contact with a person. Your authority will work in a bathroom stall, at your seat, in the middle of congregational worship, or a mall, walking through a store, or driving through a city. Know your authority and you will SHIFT people and spheres.

- Depending on your calling, God may lead you to bring correction as Peter did in Acts. Correction should not be belittling and defaming. Correction should always be done in a manner that releases empowerment, conviction and a desire for change. God will lead you on who to correct and how to correct. If He does not lead you then keep your mouth closed. Everyone cannot handle what you discern, and can only receive what you discern by the leading of God.

Purifying Our Discernment

Implement the following tools purify your discernment:

- Repent for personal sins; sins of family, region and nation

- Repent and turn from things you should not be watching and listening to

- Constantly cleanse your souls, heart, emotions, thoughts and mind with the blood, fire, and power of God

- Take consistent time to cleanse with the blood of Jesus, fire, and power of God, each of our senses: *(The keener your discernment, the more you will need to cleanse because you will be sensitive to everything and the enemy will look for avenues to contaminate your discernment)*

1.   *Sight* (cleanse your natural and spiritual eyes, the eyes of your understanding, your dream and sleep realm, and the realm where you have open visions; cleanse all natural and spiritual blindness and demonic and afflicting attacks against the eyes; command 20/20 vision spiritually and naturally and that you possess the eyes of Christ)

2.   *Hearing* (cleanse your natural and spiritual hearing, negative thoughts and perceptions that you hear yourself saying, the devil saying, or hear in the atmosphere.

105

Cleanse all deaf and dumbness and dull hearing and command keenness of hearing spiritually and naturally and a consistent inclining of your ears to the heart of God).

3.   _Touch_ (live a lifestyle of fasting so the flesh can be subjected to the Holy Spirit. Cleanse all sexual, sensual, lustful, and ungodly touches and sensations in your body, emotions, and thoughts. Cleanse any sensations that may come from hugging, touching, praying, encountering people and environments. Things at times transfer even when we do not realize it. Things transfer to attack us and provoke us to sin or for no reason at all).

4.   *Smell* (Cleanse your nose, respiratory system, sinuses and ability to smell and discern spiritually and naturally. The enemy loves to distract us with colds, sinus infections, allergies so our senses will be naturally out of whack, where we have trouble spiritually focusing and discerning properly. Who can focus and discern when they are coughing, hacking, sneezing, bound with a headache, and contested. The devil is crafty. Counterattack this by keeping this area clean of sickness and disease. As you cleanse your sense of smell you will become sharpened and thus be sensitive to all types of perfumes and smells. Be cautious of this as God could be showing you how the enemy uses these

things to bind your senses. You may have to quit wearing certain perfumes and the like).

5.   *Taste* (Cleanse yourself of ungodly desires naturally and spiritually. Cleanse yourself of all ungodly and unhealthy habits and additions naturally and spiritually. Any appetite you have that exalt itself above God cleanse it, fall out of agreement with it. Command the taste, smell, and sensation of it to be cleansed out of your heart, mind, body and soul).

- Repent, cleanse and fall out of agreement with personal judgments, opinions, pet peeves and personal quirks, critical perceptions
- Practice not giving in to personal judgments, opinions, pet peeves and personal quirks, critical perceptions but remaining silent until we have God's heart and words regarding a matter
- Repent quickly when thinking or speaking personal judgments, opinions, pet peeves and personal quirks, critical perceptions and admit that it is us speaking and not God (stop lying on God)
- Practice daily being a demonstration of God's nature, character and plan
- Practice daily speaking and sharing the gospel through God's mandate of saving (delivering, healing, rescuing), empowering,

reconciling, restoring, transforming, and drawing people to God.

As you cleanse your senses consistently and operate through the heart of God, your discernment will become sharpened and you will be extremely sensitive to people, environments, atmospheres, and world around you.

Hebrews 5:12 - But strong meat belongeth to them that are of full age, even those who by reason of use have their senses exercised to discern both good and evil.

The Amplified Version - But solid food is for full- grown men, for those whose senses and mental faculties are trained by practice to discriminate and distinguish between what is morally good and noble and what is evil and contrary either to divine or human law.

- You will sense angels, clouds of witnesses, the glory, the power of God
- You will sense deliverance, healing, transformation taking place in people, the environment, atmosphere and region
- You will sense God's protection, shielding, and force field enveloping you, others, the region
- You will sense heaven invading your sphere or as if you left earth and you are now operating from a heavenly sphere

- You will sense when you have entered heaven or heavenly realms and be able to operate in heaven
- You will sense when God has opened, or closed His heavens or when a place is cultivated (heavens remain open) for His glory
- You will sense God's nature, character, His love, His wrath, His judgment
- You will sense when God is happy, sad, grieved, pleased

- You will sense witchcraft, idolatry, demons, lust, perversion, sin attached to people, atmospheres, and situations.
- You will sense when you have entered a demonic realm, a demonic or bound place or atmosphere
- You may sense when witchcraft has been done in a place or region or when a place has been dedicated to Satan.
- You might not be able to wear certain perfumes, scents, and apparel because of what is attached to them.
- You may have challenges being in certain stores, around certain people and environments, even certain church and ministry environments.
- You will be in awe at some of the things you see and will not understand the reason people are doing what they do or the reason such things will be allowed or received.

- You will experience a righteous anger and indignation at times.
- You will be afraid of what you see as it will be scary and look so demonic and horrific that you will think you are losing your mind or just entered the twilight zone.
- You will want to tell others but they will think you are crazy because they will not understand and are not mature discerners.
- You will have a lot of secrets and talks with God because you will have only Him to share with regarding what you are sensing.

You will know keenly what is God and what is not of Him, even when people try to contend it is of God or that mixture is okay. God will be using discernment to show you His heart versus the world's heart, His plan versus the world's plan - what is of Him and what is not of Him. Stay focused and seek Him for what He is saying and may want you to do. Do not get distracted by what you discern, that hinders God's ability to use you in that moment.

Apostolic Decrees & Divine Prophesy

- Words are devices
- Words are actual physical matter going forth
- Words actually birth forth the thoughts, desires and plans of God

Psalms 92:5 - O Lord, how great are thy works! And thy thoughts are very deep.

Thoughts in the Hebrew is *"machashebeth"* and means:

1. a contrivance which means to plan with ingenuity; devise; invent
2. a texture, machine, or intention,
3. plan (whether bad, a plot; or good, advice): — cunning (work), curious work,
4. device (- sed), imagination, invented,
5. a means, purpose, work, imaginations, invention

The Message Version - How magnificent your work, God! How profound your thoughts!

The New English Translation - How great are your works, O Lord! Your plans are very intricate!

Proverbs 12:5-6 - The thoughts of the righteous are right: but the counsels of the wicked are deceit. The words of the wicked are to lie in wait for blood: but the mouth of the upright shall deliver them.

The Message Version - *The thinking of principled people makes for justice; the plots of degenerates corrupt. The words of the wicked kill; the speech of the upright saves.*

Isaiah 55:8-11 - *For my thoughts are not your thoughts, neither are your ways my ways, saith the Lord. For as the heavens are higher than the earth, so are my ways higher than your ways, and my thoughts than your thoughts. For as the rain cometh down, and the snow from heaven, and returneth not thither, but watereth the earth, and maketh bring forth and bud, that it may give seed to the sower, and bread to the eater: So shall my word be that goeth forth out of my mouth: it shall not return unto me void, but it shall accomplish that which I please, and it shall prosper in the thing whereto I sent it.*

Webster's Online Dictionary's defines "*decree*" as:

1. a formal and authoritative order, especially one having the force of law
2. a presidential decree
3. law, a judicial decision or order
4. in Theology or Christianity decree is one of the eternal purposes of God, by which events are foreordained

According to Webster's Online Dictionary, the definition of "*declare*" means:

1. the act of declaring: announcement

2. the first pleading in a common-law action : a statement made by a party to a legal transaction usually not under oath

3. something that is declared: the document containing such a declaration

My mentor, Apostle Jackie Green, says decree and declare actually means to *"announce, bomb, inform, give notice, profession, publication, report, remark, revelation, say so, testify and confirm."*

***Job 22:28** – You will also decree a thing, and it will be established for you; so light will shine on your way.*

The Amplified Version - *You shall also decide and decree a thing, and it shall be established for you; and the light [of God's favor] shall shine upon your ways.*

The Message Version - *You'll decide what you want and it will happen; your life will be bathed in light.*

The New Living Translation - *You will succeed in whatever you choose to do, and light will shine on the road ahead of you.*

<u>*Decree* in this passage of scripture is *"gazar"* and means:</u>

1. to cut, divide, cut down, cut off, cut in two, snatch, decree
2. to cut off, destroy, exterminate
3. to be cut off, separated, excluded

113

4. to be destroyed, cut off
5. to be decreed

When we decree we divide God's word
from the enemy's and man's word by
snatching down, cutting off, and destroying
or as my mentor says bombing the power,
strongholds, and limitations that prevent
God's original state for creating us in His
image from manifesting.

We exterminate a present judgment, while
establishing God's true judgment and law,
His ultimate desires for our lives before the
fall of man.

Established in this scripture is *"quwm"* and
means:
1. to rise, arise, stand, rise up, stand up
2. to arise (hostile sense)
3. to become powerful
4. to maintain oneself
5. to be established, be confirmed
6. to endure
7. to be fixed
8. to be valid
9. to be proven, ratify, impose
10. to be fulfilled, fulfill
11. to persist
12. to be set, be fixed
13. to raise, set up, erect, build
14. to come or bring on the scene
15. to rouse, stir up, investigate
16. to constitute
17. to cause to stand, set, station

18. to make binding

According to Webster's Online Dictionary, the definition of *"establish"* means:
1. to institute (as a law) permanently by enactment or agreement : settle to make firm or stable: to introduce and cause to grow and multiply
2. to bring into existence: found, bring abound, effect
3. to put on a firm basis: set up: to put into a favorable position: to gain full recognition or acceptance of
4. to make (a church) a national or state institution, to put beyond doubt : Prove

After we establish what we speak then the light of God comes and births forth what we have solidified:

Light in Hebrew is *"or"* and means:
1. illumination or (concrete) luminary (in every sense, including lightning, happiness, etc.)
2. light(s), day, bright, clear, flood, herbs, lightning, morning
3. light of day, light of heavenly
4. luminaries (moon, sun, stars), day- break, dawn, morning light
5. daylight, lightning
6. light of lamp, light of life, light of prosperity
7. light of instruction light of face (fig.) Jehovah as Israel's light

Dictionary.com definition of _"illuminate"_ is:

1. to supply or brighten with light; light up
2. to make lucid or clear; throw light on (a subject)
3. to decorate with lights, as in celebration
4. to enlighten, as with knowledge
5. to make resplendent or illustrious:

In this chapter, we have Eliphaz providing counsel to Job. Job was stripped of everything he had including family, possessions, and health, at the permission of God. Eliphaz's presumption was that Job had sinned and therefore, had caused God to judge him. Though Job had not sinned, Eliphaz was definitely correct in letting Job know that he had the power to speak life into his present situation, and God would restore and establish him greater than he was before the enemy was allowed to terrorize him.

No matter how much Job complained, his decree was God is always greater then what was occurring in his life.

Job took a stand and eventually saw the fullness of that decree rise up in his life on his behalf. We can see from this scripture and the definitions, that decreeing has the power to push us into a greater strength and fortitude that positions, carries out, and gives effect to God's defined plan and purpose for our lives.

Throughout the Bible those who made decrees were either authority figures, kings, or those who had great influence in their land (examples; Moses, David, Daniel, John, Peter, Jesus).

Whether good or bad, when a decree is made, it is a done deal. It cannot be changed, not even by the person who declares it. Another decree has to be made to override the initial decree. However, once a decree is made it is a done deal.

Elijah The Prophet Decreeing

Elijah is another great example of God using a man of authority, a prophet, to make a prophetic decree. In *1Kings 17:1*, God used Elijah to make a prophetic decree to Ahab stating,

"As the Lord God of Israel lives, whom, I serve, there will be neither dew nor rain in the next few years except at my word."

And indeed there was no rain in the land for the next few years. Following this drought, Elijah made this declaration to Ahab in *1Kings 18:41*,

"Get up, eat and drink, for there is a sound of the abundance of rain."

Elijah did not just make the decree of rain randomly. He carried out the specific orders of God first. Then he made the

117

decree of the abundance of rain.
Sometimes, specific instructions will need to be carried out before some decrees can come to pass.

Also please know that if you are called to decree and declare or operate in decreeing and declaring, it is important to guard your words. Guard yourselves from complaining, being critical or using your gifts of discernment and judgments as manipulation and witchcraft. I state this because whether you make a decree that is good or bad, it remains until you make another one to override it.

Also know that negative decrees that God did not ordain require repentance to undo. You just cannot speak a new decree and think all is well. That negative decree is still in motion and effect, it is still a law until the legal effects of the law is striped and only repentance and a turning breaks a curse or negative decree.

This is why we still see the effects of natural laws that have been overridden. Let us consider slavery as an example. Slavery has been abolished but we still have racism and slavery because there has not been any true repentance and turning in the land or among people. Even though times have progressed and cultures are more intertwined, the effects of the old law still operate even though a new law has been put in place.

As soon as Elijah made the declaration of the abundance of rain (*1Kings 18:41*), it further fulfilled his previous declaration that it would not rain again until he spoke it (*IKings 17:1*). His very words set the heavenlies in motion for rain and transformed his nation.

When Elijah stated that he heard the sound of the abundance of rain, it was a spiritual hearing. The rain had not yet manifested nor was there even a cloud in the sky. Elijah's proclamation about hearing the rain was made according to what God had spoken (go show yourself to Ahab and I will bring rain upon the earth). And according to what Elijah could "hear" through the spirit of God. He heard the rain before it was and spoke it and it became so.

Within the Spirit, Elijah could hear the rain forming and went on the top of Carmel to further intercede and position himself to receive the full manifestation of the decree. Elijah put his face between his legs and waited for the rain, while having his servant look seven times for it. What was spiritual was becoming natural and Elijah could hear it forming with unwavering expectation.

1Kings 18:42-45 - So Ahab went up to eat and to drink. And Elijah went up to the top of

Carmel; and he cast himself down upon the
earth, and put his face between his knees, And
said to his servant, Go up now, look toward the
sea. And he went up, and looked, and said, there
is nothing. And he said, Go again seven times.
And it came to pass at the seventh time, that he
said, Behold, there ariseth a little cloud out of the
sea, like a man's hand. And he said, Go up, say
unto Ahab, Prepare thy chariot, and get thee
down, that the rain stop thee not. And it came
to pass in the meanwhile, that the heaven was
black with clouds and wind, and there was a
great rain. And Ahab rode, and went to Jezreel.

There are instances where once you speak
and establish a decree, you have to contend
for it in intercession and in your actions of
faith, in order for the (miracle) the day
break of light can manifest.

- You may have to keep interceding and
  battering it.

- You may have to do a prophetic act like
  Elijah did when he went on Mount Carmel
  and positioned himself in intercession and
  in an apostolic stance until the heavenlies
  produced rain on earth.

- You have to show faith in what you know
  God is speaking about the thoughts (devise)
  he has planned in order to see its
  manifestation.

- The more you operate in your power to decree and declare, the easier it is to bring for the light - the miracles that these decrees produce. Jesus is our greatest example of seeing immediate decrees birth forth light - miracles.

Jesus Decreeing

Jesus is the ultimate example of one who knew His power and authority to decree and watch the breath of His words come to pass. All throughout His life on earth, Jesus would decree healing and miracles, and they would form right before the people. Everything Jesus said was so and came to pass. Jesus was the Word which made His presence of authority all the more powerful.

This is why it is important for us to have the Word inside us. When filled with the word, the thoughts (devises) of God that is in us can form from what God speaks through us. The following scriptures will give us a glimpse of a few of the decrees Jesus made:

- Mark 1:23-27 (Cast out unclean spirit)
- Mar 4:39 (Peace be still)
- Mat 8:6 (Healed and cast out devils with his word)
- Mat 20:16 (First shall be last and the last shall be first)
- Mar 14:28, 14:62, 16:17-118 (declares his resurrection)

- Mar 16:17-18 (Jesus declares that signs will follow believers)
- Jn 10:30 (I and my Father are one)
- Jn 11:25-26 (Jesus declares he is the resurrection and the life, etc.)
- Jn 11:43 (Lazarus come forth)
- Joh19:30 (It is finished)
- Mat 8 (Sending His word and healings occur)

Decree Versus Prophecy

Decreeing is built on *Isaiah 55:11*, which states, *"So shall my word be that goeth forth out of my mouth: it shall not return unto me void, but it shall accomplish that which I please, and it shall prosper [in the thing] whereto I sent it."*

Though some prophetic words are decrees, not every prophetic word is a decree. Prophecy is the promise, potential, and desired will of God (*See 1Corinthians 14:3*). Decreeing is the establishment of God's will, the institution of His promises. When declared through prophecy, decrees distinguish *"what is"* from *"what was,"* while providing an immediate manifestation of what will be.

Though prophecy can convey the will of God and is a set in stone word or directive, you have a choice in accepting or rejecting the word. Your choice can dictate whether God's will manifest in your life or for a particular situation. But when God makes a decree, there is no choice. "**IT IS SO!**"

Decreeing reorders us to our original state of authority, position, and dominion (emotionally, spiritually, and physically) before Adam fell. It empowers heaven on earth by releasing and merging our heavenly kingdom with our natural lives.

Purpose For Decreeing
- Covers and establishes the mantle of the word
- Immerses us in the principles of God's word
- Releases and establishes God's judgments and vengeance
- Refreshes and revitalizes prophecies that have been spoken over our lives
- Releases and dislodges those words and goods that have been stored or held up in the Spirit realm (Dan 10)
- Births forth decisions and yields conclusions to the matter at hand
- Establishes spiritual laws that bring about a natural good or necessary purpose
- Brings security in what God has said to, for, or through us

How To Decree:
Decrees must be spoken from a position of authority. One must be confident in whom he or she is in God and rooted in faith that God never goes back on His word.

Matthew 11:12 And from the days of John the Baptist until now the kingdom of heaven suffereth violence, and the violent take it by force.

We can decree through our bodies via movement, so be open to God leading you to perform a prophetic act while decreeing, or to dance or dramatize a decree. I minister this way a lot during praise and worship and in my personal time of prayer and intercession. At times, movement and prophetic acts, aide in bringing release and fullness to what God is birthing and establishing. Many of the prophets, Elijah, Ezekiel, completed prophetic acts.

What we decree MUST be the will, heart, and mind of Christ - not our desires, presumptions, or opinions.

We cannot continue to just speak things into the atmosphere and hope decrees come to pass. Decrees must be spoken within the Spirit realm. The person must enter the Spirit and command those things in the Spirit to be made flesh in their natural lives. The Spirit realm is as close as you believe it to be. If you believe it to be a matter of batting an eye, you will enter at that level of faith. If you believe the Spirit realm is far away and you have to pray it into existence, then you will enter at that level of faith. Since we are spiritual beings and are to be living spiritual lives, I would encourage you to acquire a revelation of the spirit realm being right at your disposal - right at the blink of an eye. Or that you are so enmeshed that even a blink is not necessary, as this allows you to be one with God, and increases your level of access to Him, His presence and His every kingdom good you desire or need.

I would encourage you to pray and stand on a decree until God releases your Spirit. Often we will make loose statements into the heavenlies or we will pray and make decrees concerning matters, but we end the prayer without God yielding a release in the Spirit. Though decrees are established, at times we have to battle in prayer to see them come to pass. The Holy Spirit provides a release so that we will know that what we have prayed/decreed has been taken care of and to elevate us to another level of faith. Sometimes we abort manifestation because we fail to pray without ceasing or we fail to pray through to a place of completion with God. After making your decrees, praise and worship or even wait quietly until God releases you from the prayer.

When we decree we are scribing (establishing). We are giving an account of God's goodness and ability and we are eternally publishing His works and will, and His promises and proclamations for our lives and those we minister to. God put power in our mouths, hands and feet so that

125

we could set the captives free and be establishers of His kingdom. As movers and shakers of the kingdom, we must be open to how God desires to use us and be available to decreeing His will so the fullness of our destinies and His kingdom can manifest in the earth.

Dreams & Visions

Dictionary.com defines "*dream*" as, "*a succession of images, thoughts, or emotions passing through the mind during sleep, an involuntary vision occurring to a person when awake.*"

Dreams tell a story as a sequence of events tend to occur during a dream.

Dictionary.com defines "vision" as, "*an experience in which a personage, thing, or event appears vividly or credibly to the mind, although not actually present, often under the influence of a divine or other agency.*"

A vision is when the eyes open up in our imagination and we are watching a movie. Visions can happen at any time as they can occur when a person is sleep, semi-sleep, soaking in the presence of the Lord, resting, prayer, washing dishes or while a person is wide awake and going about the day. We can also have visions within our dreams as sometimes we maybe dreaming and then a vision will manifest inside the dream.

Sometimes a person will receive mental pictures or quick flashes of people, situations, images, etc. When this happens, ask God what He is wanting you to do with what He is showing you.

Dreams, visions and mental pictures can be of God, demonic, or soulish. Some dreams, vision and mental pictures we label as demonic, could be God revealing things about the enemy, principalities and high places in the region, the end times, or could be a word of correction or warning. If you are unsure of which category the dream belongs, ask God if the dream is of Him or not. He will let you know and will lead you in what to do with the dream or vision.

God speak through dreams and visions to:

- Hide His word in our heart
- Reveal our callings and giftings (Genesis 37:5-7)
  Share revelation when we are rested that we are too busy to hear and retain during the day (Job 33:15-26)
- Provoke our Spirit to seek Him for deeper things regarding His word and presence, as dreams require us to dig deep into the mysteries of God
- Release and/or confirm prophecy (Daniel 7, Judges 7:13-14, Genesis 40:5)
- Reveal personal, generational, and regional strongholds
- Reveal future and end time revelation and happenings
- Expose the enemy's camp to us (Matthew 2:19-21)

- Reveal sin issues or warn of potential to sin (Genesis 20:3-7)
- Reveal soul wound issues to us
- Reveal truth (Matthew 27:19)
- Heal, deliver (Judges 7:13-15), warn (Genesis 20:3), empower, commune (1Kings 3:5), reconcile, restore, mend hearts and even relationships, instill reverenced fear (Job 7:14)
- Fulfill the prophecy of Joel regarding His outpouring of dreams and visions (Joel 2:28, Acts 2:17)

Daniel 1:17 - *As for these four children, God gave them knowledge and skill in all learning and wisdom: and Daniel had understanding in all visions and dreams.*
Just as Daniel, we can have access in understanding all our visions and dreams. It is important not to get frustrated when we do not receive an initial interpretation or revelation of a dream or vision. Frustration blocks us from being able to hear and discern God.

- Some dreams maybe for a specific time and God is just hiding the dream in your heart for a later day.
- Sometime we are not ready for the interpretation.
- Sometimes we may need to fast and spend time in pray for an interpretation.

- Sometimes our imagination is clogged with mixture and worldly contamination which hinders our interpretation.
- Sometimes we could have been having an actual encounter with God or we are in the spirit realm having an actual experience and no interpretation is needed.
- Sometimes we do not want to acknowledge truth so we seek interpretation when we already know what God is saying.
- Sometimes we fear the interpretation so we are resistant to hearing and being accountable to what will be required of us.
- Sometimes we second guess our interpretation because of our own inadequacy.

As someone who has constant dreams and visions, I assure you that you can read countless books on the subject and should do just that, however, the best teacher for interpreting your dreams and visions and utilizing them in life, and ministry is the Holy Spirit. I state this because there is no true pattern for interpreting dreams. The Holy Spirit may lead you to interpret one way for one dream and then entirely different way for another. The significance to interpreting dreams and visions is being sensitive to the Holy Spirit, while being able to identify the keys in the dreams and visions; and unlocking the mysteries to what the Lord is speaking.

Acts 2:17-18 - And it shall come to pass in the last days, God declares, that I will pour out of My Spirit upon all mankind, and your sons and your daughters shall prophesy [telling forth the divine counsels] and your young men shall see visions (divinely granted appearances), and your old men shall dream [divinely suggested] dreams. Yes, and on My menservants also and on My maidservants in those days I will pour out of My Spirit, and they shall prophesy [telling forth the divine counsels and predicting future events pertaining especially to God's kingdom].

Out is "*cheo*" in the Greek and means:
1. (to pour); to pour forth; figuratively, to bestow
2. gush (pour) out, run greedily (out), shed (abroad, forth), spill
3. shed, shed forth, spill, run out, run greedily, shed abroad
4. metaphor: to bestow or distribute largely

This passage let us know that God expects us to dream and have visions. God says He is pouring out His Spirit. His outpouring suggests that dreams and visions should be endlessly available to us. They should be constant and greedily run in an outpouring into our lives. With them comes prophesy and destiny downloads (dream dreams) that advance the kingdom. We should be dreaming and experiencing visions and we should be receiving answers, revelation, and direction from our dreams and visions.

It is important to understand that dreams are real realms. Science contends that we encounter five stages of rest before we actually enter deep sleep. Though science is unsure of the reason for the stages, they contend that throughout the night we can go in and out of these stages. As we enter a place of rest, our physical body goes to sleep and enters a stage of paralysis. Our brain is still active and is sending signals to our body to ensure we retain the necessary functions to maintain life as we sleep. Stage five is where we encounter REM (rapid eye movement) sleep aka as deep sleep.

Though we can have visions and dreams in other stages, the REM stage is where most dreams occur and is where our heart rate increases, as it is pumping blood to our brain and other body parts to maintain life.

Science does not speak of this, we know however, from the bible stating that God who is all Spirit (Psalms 121:3-4), never sleeps or slumbers, so our Spirit never sleeps. And we see from science that our heart is active as well. Our soul is a part of our heart and Spirit so though it can be at peace or rest, it does not sleep either. I would contend that because our heart, soul, and spirit are awake, this is the reason many dreams feel so real - like real encounters. They feel real because they are. Our heart, soul and Spirit are actively engaged in our night season though our body maybe sleep and/or at rest.

- What we expose our heart, soul and spirit to when we are awake, can help determine the realms we enter when we are asleep.
- Also, what we meditate upon before and as we press into sleep can be a factor of the realms we enter into.
- Soulish and life/heart issue can also determine the realms we are exposed to when we sleep.
- Because our defenses are down, demons, witches, astral projectors tend to attack when we are sleeping.
- And of course God can always open sleep realms to us.

Proverbs 4:20-23 - *My son, attend to my words; incline thine ear unto my sayings. Let them not depart from thine eyes; keep them in the midst of thine heart. For they are life unto those that find them, and health to all their flesh. Keep thy heart with all diligence; for out of it are the issues of life.*

Matthew 12:35 - *A good man out of the good treasure of the heart bringeth forth good things: and an evil man out of the evil treasure bringeth forth evil things.*

During REM sleep or deep sleep, we are in our most vulnerable realm. I say this because, our body has gone through the process of being at to total rest, and our

133

brain has entered a state where mainly the eyes are active. The eyes is where our imagination is housed. The bible tells us to cast down vain imagination and everything that exalts itself about Him.

2Corinthians 10:4-6 - *(For the weapons of our warfare are not carnal, but mighty through God to the pulling down of strong holds); Casting down imaginations, and every high thing that exalteth itself against the knowledge of God, and bringing into captivity every thought to the obedience of Christ.*

We assume we are not to have an imagination or we cannot use our imagination. This is error. Imagination is the realm where God speaks to us through dreams, visions, and pictures. It is also the place where we mediate on the image and things of a God.

Psalms 1:2 - *But his delight [is] in the law of the LORD; and in his law doth he meditate day and night.*

Philippians 4:8 - *Finally, brethren, whatsoever things are true, whatsoever things [are] honest, whatsoever things [are] just, whatsoever things [are] pure, whatsoever things [are] lovely, whatsoever things [are] of good report; if [there be] any virtue, and if [there be] any praise, think on these things.*

Psalms 1:1-2 - Blessed [is] the man that walketh not in the counsel of the ungodly, nor standeth in the way of sinners, nor sitteth in the seat of the scornful. But his delight [is] in the law of the LORD; and in his law doth he meditate day and night.

The eyes is where our imagination is stored and is where our dreams, visions, and mental pictures occur. As we meditate, our imagination begins to fill up with God images – His character and His nature – and then God begins to use our imagination to download His plan to us through visions and dreams. When our imagination is full of vain glory, worldliness, wickedness, and when we have not effectively meditated and focused on God, He cannot give us His thoughts, pictures, dreams, visions. Our imagination will be consumed with things that are not of Him, and that exalt against the knowledge of who He is in our lives.

Ephesians 1:18 - The eyes of your understanding being enlightened; that ye may know what is the hope of his calling, and what the riches of the glory of his inheritance in the saints.

Eyes is "*ophthalmos*" in the Greek and means, "*vision, the eyes of the mind, the faculty of knowing.*"

Enlightened is _"photizo"_ in the Greek and means:

1. to give light, to shine
2. to enlighten, light up, illumine
3. to bring to light, render evident
4. to cause something to exist and thus come to light and become clear to all
5. to enlighten, spiritually, imbue with saving knowledge
6. to instruct, to inform, teach, to give understanding to

Our eyes is where we can discern, know, and see, the path of God. As we are consistently enlighten by mediating (imaging) on the things of God, we are being consumed and activated in His riches and calling for our lives. This is essential to a life of a prayer warrior. Because it will enable the prayer warrior to discern which dreams and visions are from God and which are not. It will also assist the prayer warrior with being able to discern the keys in a dream/vision that are necessary for interpreting and effectively applying what is being revealed to life situations.

When interpreting dreams, visions, mental pictures pay attention to the follow:

- Journal all your dreams/visions, even the demonic and soulish ones. There could be clues in them to thwart the dreams/visions from occurring again

- Though not always the case, a dream can be two or three dimensional. Be open to exploring the dream from these three areas:
  - How it relates to the person having the dream
  - How it relates to the people and situations in the dream
  - How it relates to the body of Christ and world at large
- Colors (study biblical colors and learn what they mean
- What is occurring in the dream and vision (journal even the little things that you would normally think do not matter – they may hold the greatest keys)
- Who is in the dream/vision (dogs, momma, friend, strangers)
- What were the names (what is the definition of their names –use online search engines to acquire the definition of their name)
- What was in the dream/vision (cars, houses, pictures)
- What was the time of day in the dream/vision and when the dream/vision occurred (morning, noon, night)
- Season the dream/vision took place (winter, spring, summer, fall)
- Where did the dream take place (Texas, in a church, at a park)
- Mood of the dream (gloomy, happy, sunny)
- Mood and characteristics of the person dreaming and those in the dream (happy, sad, depressed, confused, suspicious, controlling, angry)

- Does the dream/vision confirm, reveal, warn, expose, encourage, discourage, set free, bind up, etc.
- What are your initial thoughts when first awaking from the dream, as you journal the dream, and after further exploring the dream
- What scriptures come to mind as you consider the dream/vision
- What experiences, people, situations, places, etc., come to mind as you explore the dream/vision
- Use wisdom on who to acquire interpretation or further exploration of the dream/vision from. It is okay to seek assistance interpreting a dream/vision but make sure it is someone you trust and that is mature in their walk. It can also be someone who has the gift of interpretation
- Only share the dream/vision as the Spirit leads. Sometimes, it is not necessary to share a dream/vision with a person or congregation. Simply share the message or strategy given in a dream/vision. Everyone will not be able to handle what occurred in the dream/vision and it could be a factor with them receiving what God is striving to convey. Seek God regarding what He reveals to you in a dream/vision and follow through with what He says
- When God shows you dreams/visions about your calling and future, be cautious who you share them with. You expect everyone to be happy for you but this is not

reality. Joseph's brother threw him in a pit and then sold him into slavery when he shared his dreams with them. If you are just burning to tell someone talk to Jesus about it; though He already knows, He will be happy for you and even empower you in what He has revealed to you (laughing but very serious)

- If you are unsure about something regarding a dream/vision or forget a part, do not make assumptions or add to the dream/vision. Ask God to reveal the information to you and be okay if He desires not to. Sometimes this information is hidden in your heart for a later season and so God only allows you to remember what is necessary for the present season.
- Revisit your dreams/visits as some dreams and visions can mean one thing in one season and have a whole other meaning in another season of your life, the people life that is in the dream/vision or for the body of Christ and world as a whole

Godly & Demonic Visitation

It is important to govern our dream and vision realms and to learn how to be interactive in our dreams and visions. This will enable to us:

- to commune with God in our dreams and visions
- to know when God is wanting us to get up and war and intercede
- to know when dreams and visions are not of God, are demonic in nature and that the enemy is infiltrating our dreams to attack us
- to know when we are having a divine visitation from God versus having a dream or vision
- to know when we are experiencing a demonic visitation from devils, ghosts, astral projectors, sex demons, terrors (fear demons), destiny killers (demons sent to kill or cause us to self-destruct) versus having a dream or vision

In *1Kings 3:5-13*, we find Solomon responding and making his desires known to God in a dream.

In Gibeon the Lord appeared to Solomon in a dream by night: and God said, Ask what I shall give thee. And Solomon said, Thou hast shewed unto thy servant David my father great mercy, according as he walked before thee in truth, and in righteousness, and in uprightness of heart

140

*with thee; and thou hast kept for him this great
kindness, that thou hast given him a son to sit
on his throne, as it is this day. And now, O
Lord my God, thou hast made thy servant king
instead of David my father: and I am but a little
child: I know not how to go out or come in.*

*And thy servant is in the midst of thy people
which thou hast chosen, a great people, that
cannot be numbered nor counted for multitude.
Give therefore thy servant an understanding
heart to judge thy people, that I may discern
between good and bad: for who is able to judge
this thy so great a people? And the speech
pleased the Lord, that Solomon had asked this
thing. And God said unto him, Because thou
hast asked this thing, and hast not asked for
thyself long life; neither hast asked riches for
thyself, nor hast asked the life of thine enemies;
but hast asked for thyself understanding to
discern judgment;*

*Behold, I have done according to thy words: lo, I
have given thee a wise and an understanding
heart; so that there was none like thee before
thee, neither after thee shall any arise like unto
thee. And I have also given thee that which thou
hast not asked, both riches, and honour: so that
there shall not be any among the kings like unto
thee all thy days.*

In constantly meditating upon God and
perfecting His image within our
imagination, we can discern and respond to
God's voice even when we are sleeping and

dreaming, and we are able to commune with Him. God gives me a lot of strategies for ministry assignments, ways to combat the enemy, and even answers and prophetic words in my sleep and dreams. I am able to get up and write them down and return to communing with God and even back to sleep. This is because I have cultivated this part of my life with God. I expect God to talk to me even in my sleep. Sometimes, I ask Him to speak to me in dreams and visions or just to commune with me as I sleep. Because I am expecting to hear from God, my Spirit is activated to respond and I do not see it as an inconvenience when I have to get up and journal, prayer, or fellowship further with God.

It is important to note that God will also use us in dreams and visions to war and combat the enemy. God will also take us in the heavenlies at night to war and intercede.

Ephesians 6:12 - *For we wrestle not against flesh and blood, but against principalities, against powers, against the rulers of the darkness of this world, against spiritual wickedness in high places.*

<u>High is "epouranios" in the Greek and means:</u>
1. above the sky, celestial, heavenly, high
2. existing in the heaven, things that take place in the heaven
3. the heavenly regions
a. heaven itself, the abode of God and angels

b. the lower heavens, of the stars,
c. the heavens, of the clouds
4. the heavenly temple or sanctuary
5. of heavenly origin or nature

Sometimes God will require us to armor up and literally enter the heavenlies to contend with these high places. God will lead us in war and intercession through dream and vision realms or by actually SHIFTING us into the heavenlies to combat these forces.

If you are like me, you may have had experiences of being in the heavenlies and in high places but not know the reason or purpose. This has caused great warfare, confuse, demonic attacks and even caused fear of going to sleep, praying, and not wanting to be used of God. This is an area in the body of Christ where teaching is needed so we will know that God does use us in this nature, and that He can teach us how to operate in the heavenlies to take down these high places for His glory.

If you are like me, today I cleanse and break you of your frustration, false or misperceived mental illness, hurt from people and warfare, and SHIFT you into knowing that this is part of your calling and God wants to use you powerfully to beat devils and wickedness down. I declare the revelation in this chapter will SHIFT you into the victor and successful kingdom ambassador of every realm that is attached to your destiny.

Even as God will use us to contend with the enemy, the enemy will also attack us in dreams and visions and through demonic visitations. It important to learn when it is God releasing information about the demonic realm through visions and dreams, and when it is the enemy attacking. It is also important to learn how to counterattack, and even to be proactive in our dreams to avoid attacks.

I have a lot of dreams and visions that reveal secrets, revelations, and strategies about the enemy's camp and how to infiltrate those strongholds. These are not sweet precious dreams. They are usually filled with witches, covens, high places, demons, evil people, and border on being nightmares. I would attest that I could write my own horror movies and put Hollywood to shame.

Many in the body of Christ are having these same dreams and visions, but are ruling them as nightmares and/or of no relevance because we have been taught that God would not allow us to have such dreams. I use to think that too until I kept having them. At times, I would not just have dreams but be in the spirit realm, visiting these locations, combating demons and witches and on and on. When I would share my experiences, many would contend I was possessed or mentally ill. As I have considered this over the years, I believe many are misdiagnosed as mentally ill.

They have similar experiences as I have, but because there is no or minimal teaching and a fear of exploring such revelation, we medicate and bind up people to try to stop these experiences rather than search God regarding them.

Proverbs 3:24-26 - *When thou liest down, thou shalt not be afraid: yea, thou shalt lie down, and thy sleep shall be sweet. Be not afraid of sudden fear, neither of the desolation of the wicked, when it cometh. For the Lord shall be thy confidence, and shall keep thy foot from being taken.*

The word *fear* in this scripture is *"pahad"* in the Hebrew and means, *"sudden alarm, terror, dread, great dread, an object or thing of dread."*

The Amplified Version
When you lie down, you shall not be afraid; yes, you shall lie down, and your sleep shall be sweet. Be not afraid of sudden terror and panic, nor of the stormy blast or the storm and ruin of the wicked when it comes [for you will be guiltless], for the Lord shall be your confidence, firm and strong, and shall keep your foot from being caught [in a trap or some hidden danger].

In this passage of scripture God promises that if we are not afraid when we lie down, our sleep will be sweet. He encourages us to not be afraid (startled, alarmed, caught off guard) of sudden terror and panic. And that He will even keep our foot firm and from being overtaken.

- **These terrors can be a demon, sudden fear due to challenging situations, or just a panic of fear that hits us out of nowhere.**
- **These sudden terrors can come during the day and also at night while we are sleeping.**
- **The Hebrew word for** *foot* **is** *"regel"* **and means** *"to be able to endure, haunt, journey, keep pace."* **These terrors come to haunt us, steal our journey; prevent us from keeping pace in God. They will try to kill and overtake us and hinder, thwart, and scar us from walking in the calling that is on our lives or even just functioning daily in life.**
- **These terrors will make us feel as though we have done something wrong, but God tells us** *"you will be guiltless."*

If you are not participating in any unrepentant sin, witchcraft and idolatry that may cause these attacks to occur, knowing you are guiltless is important when experiencing these attacks. I say this because the enemy and people will make you feel like you have done something wrong or opened a door, and that is the

146

reason they are occurring. I have been accused of all kinds of things in my effort to acquire deliverance from demonic dreams, visions, and demonic night attacks and visitations. These accusations only caused me to be more fearful, more frustrated, and angry with people who should have been able to help me, and with God who I expected to deliver and protect me. I had to realize that these attacks and encounters where due to and a part of the calling on my life. When I received and accepted that revelation, I begin to cleanse myself of the anger, condemnation, and shame and guilt that I carried. Then with the help of the Holy Spirit, I begin to teach myself how to reign over my night and dream realms and be proactive in my attacks against the enemy.

Psalms 91:1-6

He that dwelleth in the secret place of the most High shall abide under the shadow of the Almighty. I will say of the Lord, He is my refuge and my fortress: my God; in him will I trust. Surely he shall deliver thee from the snare of the fowler, and from the noisome pestilence. He shall cover thee with his feathers, and under his wings shalt thou trust: his truth shall be thy shield and buckler. Thou shalt not be afraid for the terror by night; nor for the arrow that flieth by day; Nor for the pestilence that walketh in darkness; nor for the destruction that wasteth at noonday.

In *Psalms 91*, David is declaring that he dwells in the secret place (covering) and shadow (presence) of God. This secret place and shadow possess:

- God's protective wings (feathers)
- God's covering (refuge)
- God's force field or hedge (fortress)
- God's revelation (shield)
- God's truth (buckler)

David is also declaring that because of God's covering and presence, he will be delivered from and will not fear:

- the snare of the fowler (traps)
- the noisome pestilence (aggravating and pesky demons and experiences)
- the pestilence that walk in darkness (sicknesses, afflictions, demons, ghosts, astral projectors which are people witches, warlocks who translate themselves in the spirit realm to do harm or for thrills, evil lurking in the dark or behind the scenes of life)
- the terror by night (fear, dread, demons and situations that haunt us)
- arrows that fly during the day (situations, word curses, witchcraft, demonic attacks that hit out of nowhere and for no apparent reason)
- the destruction that waste at noon day (situations and demons that come to cause you to destruct)

Since David is in the secret place, what reason does he have to remind himself or make a declaration that God will surely deliver him and that he should have no fear? That's a great question. I was challenged by the realization of what David was experiencing despite being in the secret place (covering) and shadow (presence) of God.

One of the things I learned from life and *Psalms 91* is that snares, pestilences, terror, arrows, and efforts of destruction are inevitable. Because of the increase of wickedness in the world, we can expect them to continually be a part of the world. We do not like to be afraid, attacked or to feel that we lack control what happens to us. Though we live in this world and can be affected by the challenges of this world, we are not of this world (*Ephesians 2:6-7...we are seated in heavenly places with Christ Jesus*). We therefore, have to change our mindsets and approach to the experiences of this world, so we can avoid being overtaken by fear and dread of them occurring.

John 16:33 - *These things I have spoken unto you, that in me ye might have peace. In the world ye shall have tribulation: but be of good cheer; I have overcome the world.*

New Living Translation - *These things I have spoken to you, so that in Me you may have peace. In the world you have tribulation, but take courage; I have overcome the world.*

We have to SHIFT from a position of worrying and dreading, to knowing that terror and tribulation resides in the world, yet God is all around us and has us. The more we *"take courage"* and yield less to fear and dread, the more we will experience God's peace, covering, protection, deliverance, refuge, fortress. We do this by consistently practicing a lifestyle of courage, while trusting and receiving God's shield (revelation) and buckler (truth). God has overcome the world and has control over every situation in our lives.

Psalms 91:9-12 - *Because thou hast made the Lord, which is my refuge, even the most High, thy habitation. There shall no evil befall thee, neither shall any plague come nigh thy dwelling. For he shall give his angels charge over thee, to keep thee in all thy ways. They shall bear thee up in their hands, lest thou dash thy foot against a stone.*

Dictionary.com defines *"befall"* as:
1. To happen or occur
2. To come as by right
3. To happen to, especially by chance or fate.

From this definition we can contend that because God is our refuge and habitation, nothing is happening to us without God knowing it or without His permission. We

see further in the scripture that God even
has angels directly assign to further guard
and uphold us.

As we sleep at night, the enemy will attack
us with nightmarish dreams and demonic
visitations but he is already defeated. He is
also a coward for waiting until we are sleep
to pounce on us. That alone let us know
that the enemy is afraid of us and knows he
really only can agitated and instill fear in us.
He has no power to overtake us as if he did,
he would not have to hit us when we are
sleep or when we least expect it.

*1Peter 5:8-10 - Keep a cool head. Stay alert. The
Devil is poised to pounce, and would like
nothing better than to catch you napping. Keep
your guard up. You're not the only ones
plunged into these hard times. It's the same with
Christians all over the world. So keep a firm grip
on the faith.*

**Devils are defeated! God has me and is for
me! I reign in God and every devil is
cowering in agony under my feat!**

Kingdom Awareness Regarding Dreams, Visions and Demonic Attacks

This chapter will discuss demons and considerations to be aware of regarding dreams, visions and demonic attacks.

- *Shapeshifters* – are demons that can change their form to appear as any person living, dead, or fictional. Initially, shapeshifters appear harmless (cats turning into lions and attacking) or even look like someone you know. It will then turn into a demon or evil thing in the dream and attack you. Shapeshifters are very subtly in dreams and tend to attack when they get you to a place of trusting them or thinking you are safe and have no reason to be alarmed. Be discerning as shapeshifters will attempt to draw you to places in a dream where you will be harmed, attacked, or all of a sudden you are being chased and running for your life.

- *Familiar Spirits* that work in dreams and visions look like someone you know, but really are a demons. Though familiar spirits will look and sound familiar, they will not have the character or personality of the person you know, will not act the way the person would normally act. They will be trying to get you to do things that are contrary to God or to what is for you, and will not be for you in the dream.

- *Witch (female sorceress) - Warlock (male sorcerer)* - Witches and warlocks tend to release their spells and attacks in the night. They use translation and astral projection to enter the heavenlies to work their spells and bind people. You may encounter a witch or warlock when God leads you to go into the heavenlies to intercede and pray. Witches and warlocks will immediately attack you when they see you. They are territorial, and will attempt to assert authority over their sphere of influence. They will see the light of God in you and assume you are there to judge them or overtake their sphere. They will attack in effort to protect themselves. Some witches and warlocks will repent and even give their life to God. Some will be sold out to the devil and will stand their ground and fight. Ask God to lead you in how to deal with witches and warlocks.
- God may have you cast them out of the heavenlies
- God may have you physically fight them
- God may tell you to have them repent and give their life to Him as He may want to use them for the kingdom
- God may tell you to have them decide whether they choose to repent or die as in the bible God has little tolerance for witches and warlocks – *"Exodus 2:18 18 Thou shalt not suffer a witch to live."* Some witches and

153

warlocks are sold out for Satan and will choose death because they will refuse to repent. Be sensitive to what God is leading you to do and do not be afraid - for greater is God's power in you than in them.

- *Astral Projectors* - witches, warlocks, or regular people who separate their soul from their physical bodies so they can travel around the heavenly realms. Though demons can attack you sexually at night, sometimes these attacks are astral projectors. They are real people translating themselves into the spirit realm to rape and molest people. They do this for thrills or just because, or to feed an altar or satanic power. Sometimes, when people have encounters in their home where they see shadows, figures of people, or things moving around, these are not always what we call ghosts or demonic entities. Astral Projectors love to scare and play tricks on people. They are thrill seekers at the expense of the general public who like to act as if these type of experiences only occur in movies. As you become keener in discernment, and being interactive in your dreams, you will be able to discern whether you are dealing with demons or astral projectors. Most astral projectors will flee if you threaten to cut their silver cord. The cord is what connects their soul to their body and they can literally die if they are disconnected from it. They also flee from rebukes in Jesus name and the blood of Jesus. If they do not respond to a rebuke or threat of cutting their cord, they are most likely a ghost or a territorial spirit that has some connection to that region or place. This would require a cleansing of the land and building to rid of these attacks.

Ecclesiastes 12:5-7 Also when they shall be afraid of that which is high, and fears shall be in the way, and the almond tree shall flourish, and the grasshopper shall be a burden, and desire shall fail: because man goeth to his long home, and the mourners go about the streets: Or ever the silver cord be loosed, or the golden bowl be broken, or the pitcher be broken at the fountain, or the wheel broken at the cistern. Then shall the dust return to the earth as it was: and the spirit shall return unto God who gave it.

- *Spiritual Weapons* - Sometimes you may require spiritual weapons to combat in your dreams and visions or when God use you in the heavenlies.

2Corinthians:10-4 – For the weapons of our warfare are not carnal, but mighty through God to the pulling down of strong holds.

New International Version - The weapons we fight with are not the weapons of the world. On the contrary, they have divine power to demolish strongholds.

155

<u>*Weapon* in the Greek is *"hoplon"* and means:</u>
1. Utensil or tool (offensive for war)
2. Armor, an instrument
3. Any tool or implement for preparing a thing arms used in warfare
4. Arms used in warfare, weapons

<u>*Warfare* in the Greek is *"strateia"* and means:</u>
1. Military service, i. e. (figuratively) the apostolic career (as one of hardship and danger): — warfare.
2. An expedition, campaign, military service, warfare
3. Paul likens his contest with the difficulties that oppose him in the discharge of his apostolic duties, as warfare

- Moses had a rod
- Ezekiel had the power of clapping hands
- Joshua had treading feet
- David had worship and the power to decree and declare – He had five smooth stones
- In the bible God has used or has threatened to use hail, fire, torrent winds, swords, scalpels, threshing instruments and on and on
- Jesus had to word and was the word and carried the government of God upon His shoulders
- We all have literal swords and the sword of the word

All through the bible we see how songs, sounds, dance and movement, praise, shouts, claps, rods, decreeing, scepters, etc., are used in warfare. God uses the foolish things to confound the wise (*1 Corinthians 1:27, Psalms 8:2*). Though God can use fleshly instruments, His weapons embody His spiritual nature and character. This means that the weapons God gives us, manifests from the spirit realm and from the reality and truth of who He is. Not from the world, our flesh, or our truth or perception. God's weapons manifest from His truth and His Spirit. (My book entitled, "*Atmosphere Changers*" yields revelation on weapons used in warfare and intercession).

Ask God to assign weapons to you and do not be afraid to call for weapons in your dreams and visions, when in the heavenlies, and during times of warfare and intercession. This is important as the devil will be threatening you with knives, guns, swords, and weapons you never seen before. But God's weapons are greater and He has even bigger and more advanced knives, guns, swords, etc. God can do great things with the simplest of weapons, so do not limit or box Him.

Jeremiah 51:20 - Thou art my battle axe and weapons of war: for with thee will I break in pieces the nations, and with thee will I destroy kingdoms.

English Standard Version
You are my hammer and weapon of war: with
you I break nations in pieces; with you I destroy
kingdoms;

The Message Version *- God says, You,*
Babylon, are my hammer, my weapon of war. I'll
use you to smash godless nations, use you to
knock kingdoms to bits.

God's weapons are for the purposes of
smashing, judging, destroying,
demolishing, extinguishing, and
dismantling strongholds, while conquering
over the enemy.

God will use us and the very fashion of
movement and expression of our existence
as war club - a battle axe, to bring about His
purpose and justice.

Battle axe in the Hebrew is *"mapes"* and
means *"a smiter, war club, club, a hammer."*

Isaiah 41:15-16 *- Behold, I will make thee a*
new sharp threshing instrument having teeth:
thou shalt thresh the mountains, and beat them
small, and shalt make the hills as chaff. Thou
shalt fan them, and the wind shall carry them
away, and the whirlwind shall scatter them: and
thou shalt rejoice in the Lord, and shalt glory in
the Holy One of Israel.

Prophetically and even naturally,
mountains are high places or positions and

thoughts of pride and idol worship. God is saying I will transform you into a threshing sledge that has teeth and you will trample and tear down mountains (the high places that exalt against me). And then you will use your hand to fan (disperse, winnow) the mountains. Your fanning hand -winding arms, shall be like a wind, even a whirlwind - a hurricane that scatters the mountains for my glory. Whewwwwww!

Even as God use us as weapons, He has a **storehouse of artillery**.

Jeremiah 50:25 NLT - The LORD has opened his armory and brought out weapons to vent his fury. The terror that falls upon the Babylonians will be the work of the Sovereign LORD of Heaven's Armies.

The Amplified Version - The Lord has opened His armory and has brought forth [the nations who unknowingly are] the weapons of His indignation and wrath, for the Lord God of hosts has work to do in the land of the Chaldeans.

NET Bible - I have opened up the place where my weapons are stored. I have brought out the weapons for carrying out my wrath. For I, the Lord GOD who rules over all, have work to carry out in the land of Babylonia.

The Message Version Verse 25-26
I, God, opened my arsenal. I brought out my weapons of wrath.

The Master, God –of–the–Angel–Armies, has a
job to do in Babylon.
Come at her from all sides! Break into her
granaries! Shovel her into piles and burn her
up. Leave nothing! Leave no one!

I believe this storehouse - arsenal of
artillery, resides in us through the Holy
Spirit as well as in heaven. **ASK GOD FOR
WEAPONS! The devil cannot handle
God's arsenal.**

- Sometimes when you wake up from dreams
  or demonic attacks, you may feel fearful,
  panicky, tired, drained, filthy, sick,
  confused, disoriented, bound, depressed,
  lonely, worried, lustful, sexually aroused,
  etc. None of these attributes are of God.
  Use the blood of Jesus and the fire of God to
  cleanse yourself as these negative attributes
  have been deposited in your soul, mind,
  emotion, and body while you dreamed or
  slept, and can affect your day to day life.
  You will be trying to figure out why you
  feel scared or panicky; it maybe because you
  spent the night being chased in your dream.
  Cleanse these things from your soul, mind,
  emotions and body so they will not have
  any control over you when you are awake.

Being Proactive & Asserting Authority Over Dreams, Visions and Attacks

- Practice a lifestyle respecting that fear is a part of life but that you do not have to be fearful. Practice a lifestyle being courageous, keeping cool, firm in the faith, and not dreading the experience of demonic dreams and visions and demonic attacks. The enemy feeds on our fear and frustration. These negative attributes can become a door opener to breeding more unnecessary attacks.
  - Consistently declare out scriptures and pray prayers that build up your identity and authority regarding who you are in God
  - Be careful what you watch and listen to and be open to giving up whatever is necessary that will open doors to unnecessary attacks and demonic dreams
  - Be proactive in maintaining and cultivating the presence of God and an open heaven over your life and home
  - When traveling, take time pray over the room you will sleep in. Some of your attacks could be because you are susceptible to demons in the territory, things that happened before you entered place or region, or because of other peoples' issues.

- Accept that Godly dreams, visions and Holy Spirit encounters are a part of your walk as a believer.

- Command your Spirit to be sensitive to God and to hearing His voice and experiencing His presence as you sleep.

- Expect to have encounters with God. As you lay down to sleep every night, soak yourself in the blood of Jesus and power of God, and as you meditate upon Him, ask Him for prophetic dreams and visions and divine downloads as you sleep. Be okay with getting up to pray, journal, and further commune as God leads you. Trust that if God gets you up, He will sustain you where you can still function and be refreshed during the day.

- Though we do not accept demonic dreams and attacks, it is important to accept everything that may come with our calling. Jesus had to accept that He was going to be persecuted and die on the cross for our sins. Paul had to accept a thorn in his side. I had to accept that God was allowing these experiences so I would one day share this information with you and be prepared and prepare others for end time warfare. (**Romans 8:18** - *For I reckon that the sufferings of this present time are not worthy to be compared with the glory which shall be revealed in us*). Ask God to give you understanding regarding the reason this is a part of your calling and to teach you how to assert authority in this area of your life.

- As you are meditating on God, command your brain and Spirit to remember and retain all dreams and visions.

- Pray against the spirit of the dream stealer who comes and zaps your dreams, preventing you from remembering them.

- Declare to your body, soul and mind that you will not fear demonic activity, but will remain in a place of peace and courage, while asserting all authority over the enemy when asleep or awake.

- Command your Spirit to be so sensitive to the atmosphere around you and that you will immediately wake up and be in a place of confident authority when a demon, witch, warlock, or astral projector is present.

- Also declare that even if you are attacked while sleep, you will not respond in fear. Declare that you will SHIFT to a posture of peace and confidence, while commanding whatever is attacking you to loose you and to be immediately cast out of your sphere of influence in Jesus name.

- After being attacked in your sleep, cleanse yourself of all fear and anything else the enemy attempts to impart into you. Many sexual attacks come to instill lust, perverse thoughts and desires, shame and guilt. Cleanse out these impurities and command your righteousness to be restored in Jesus name.

- As God leads you, counterattack any devil, witch, warlock, astral projector that attacked you in your sleep. I will add some scriptures at the end of the chapter that you can use as God leads to BAM the devil. Send angels to judge and war against devils that attack you. Using the blood of Jesus and the fortress (force field) of God, close up any doors, portals, gateways, to which demons maybe entering. If necessary, repent for any sin that caused open doors and judge every illegal attack by letting devils, witches, etc., know they are illegal and you torment them for their actions in Jesus name.

- Command your Spirit to be active and interactive in your dreams and visions. Declare that as you dream, you will be fully aware of what is occurring and will be so keen in your dreams that you will discern all familiar spirits and shapeshifters.

- If you find yourself running or being chased in your dreams, command your spirit to take authority in the dream and to stop running. Remember fear is not your portion. Because dreams occur in real realms, you have the power to assert authority over dreams and change them. Depending on what is going on in a dream,

I will call for angelic assistance, chase whatever was chasing me, and beat down whatever attacking me. I may also command myself to wake up, especially if I feel I am unsafe in a dream. I then cleanse myself of all fear, anxiety, and any traumatic events or tragedy the enemy is trying to instill in my life, and then I will ask God to send angels to deal with what occurred in the dream, while praying against whatever was attacking me in my dream.

- Some dreams manifest in real life because we do not counterattack them in prayer. Immediately cancel all demonic words and assignments in dreams involving accidents, tragedies, death attempts, loss of jobs, houses, income, health issues, etc.

Sweet Sleep Declaration

Psalms 91

*I dwell in the secret place of the most High and
abide under the shadow of the Almighty. I say of
LORD, You are my refuge and my fortress: my
God; in You I trust. Surely you have deliver me
from the snare of the fowler, and from the
noisome pestilence. You have covered me with
You feathers, and under Your wings I do trust:
Your truth is my shield and buckler. I am not
afraid of the terror by night; nor for the arrow
that flieth by day; Nor for the pestilence that
walketh in darkness; nor for the destruction that
wasteth at noonday. A thousand has fallen at
my side, and ten thousand at my right hand; but
it will not come nigh me. Only with my eyes do
I behold and see the reward of the wicked.*

*Because I have made You LORD, which is my
refuge, even the most High, my habitation; there
shall no evil befall me, neither shall any plague
come nigh my dwelling. For You Lord have
given your angels charge over me, to keep me in
all my ways. They bear me up in their hands,
lest I dash my foot against a stone.*

*I tread upon the lion and adder: the young lion
and the dragon I trample under feet. Because I
hath set my love upon You God, You have
delivered me: You have set me on high, because I*

166

know Your name. When I call upon You, You answer me: You have and will deliver me out of trouble; You have honored me and shown me the protection and covering of your salvation.

1. As a *Kingdom Heir,* I decree that I have power over all the power of the enemy whether awake, sleep, in my dreams, and within the spirit realm (Luke 10:19).
2. For I undoubtedly know that weapons of my warfare are not carnal, but mighty through God to the pulling down of strongholds. Even in my sleep, I cast down imaginations, and every high thing that exalts itself against the knowledge of God, and bring into captivity every thought, intent, devise, and action to the obedience of Christ (2Corinthians 10:4).
3. I decree I am well balanced, temperate, sober of mind, vigilant and cautious at all times, even when asleep; such that my enemy can't seize upon me to devour my destiny (1Peter 5:8).
4. I stand on Isaiah 54:17 and declare that no weapon that is formed against me shall prosper, in season or out of season, when I am sleep or in a place of rest; and contend that the Lord eternally condemns every tongue, instrument, and demonic entity that rise against me. This is my heritage because I am a servant of You, Lord.
5. I assert my God given authority as a *Kingdom Heir,* and decree a keen sensitivity to detect dangers seen and unseen. I decree

that just as in everyday life, I have power to perpetually arrest, disrupt, and halt ungodly dreams and demonic attacks; even to the point of taking immediate authority within my dreams and the spirit realm, while changing and shifting them to a place of deliverance, healing, and victory.

6. When I lie down, I am not afraid; yes, I shall lie down, and my sleep will be sweet. Whether asleep or awake, I am not afraid neither of sudden terror and panic, nor of stormy blasts or the storm and ruin of the wicked. For You Lord are my confidence, firm and strong, and You are keeping my destiny from being caught in demonic and soulish traps or hidden dangers of the enemy (Proverbs 3:23-26).

7. I repent for sins personally and generationally; sins committed in my household, upon my land, and sphere of influence. I close all doors spiritually and naturally to nightmares, generational idolatry, familiar spirits, night terrors, the boogieman, ghosts, invaders, feeders, perversion, rape, and molestation spirits, night visitors, witches, warlocks, astral projectors and demonic attackers, spirits of death and hell, demonic harassment and stranglers (Matthew 5:25).

8. I receive forgiveness and decree a freeing from all anxiousness, worry, fear, stress, anger, hatred, unforgiveness, uncleanness, trauma, etc., and decree a cleansing and freeing from any soulish and emotional areas that would give way to the enemy.

9. For I do not fret or have any anxiety about anything, but in every circumstance and in everything, by prayer and petition (definite requests), with thanksgiving, I continue to make my wants known to my God. And my God's peace has become a tranquil state within my soul. I am assured of my salvation through Christ. And so fearing nothing and being content with my Kingly inheritance, I decree that His peace, which transcends all understanding is garrisoning and mounting a powerful guard over my heart and mind and is brooding wholeness and wellness in me. (Philippians 4:6-7).

10. I therefore cancel all dedications, covenants, rituals, hexes, vexes, enchantments, bewitchments made to demons and idols, witches, warlocks, wicked people, as it relates to me personally, generationally, my land and sphere of influence, and the spiritual gifts in my family lineage (Numbers 4:18).

11. I close every, door, gateway and portal, spiritually and naturally, to demonic dreams, astral projection and my spirit man being subjected to ungodly summons in the night. I fully resist the devil and decree I only harken to the unction and voice of my King Jesus (James 4:7).

12. I plead the blood of Jesus over me, my home, my bed, my covers, my atmosphere, my possessions and sphere of influence and decree that to the pure, in heart and conscience, all things are pure (Titus 1:15).

13. As born again *Kingdom Heir*, I decree I am covered by the purified blood of Jesus and solidified in the all-powerful name of Jesus - the name that is above every name - the name to which every knee shall bow and every tongue should confess that My Jesus is Lord and savior unto the glory of God my Father, Refuge, Shelter, and Protector (Philippians 2:8-11).

14. Even now I cleanse my body, mind, spirit, soul, thoughts, emotions, personality, character, will, and sphere of influence of all tragedy, infirmity, affliction, fear, worry, weariness, tiredness, frustration, failure, depression, loneliness, double mindedness, unbelief, perversion, demonic seeds, pollution, imprints, impressions (*speak forth whatever negative attributes have been planted through dreams and demonic night attacks*). I decree a complete cleansing and healing through the blood of Jesus and the matchless name of Jesus and command every seed, root, manifestation, harvest, stench and stain of these ungodly attributes to be annulled. You are destroyed, rendered powerless and zapped to nothing by the declarative name of Jesus (Proverbs 23:7).

15. For there is no torment in love. God grants sleep to those He loves. I am consumed by God's perfect love which causes Him to sustain and comfort me as I sleep (1 John 4:18, Psalms 42:8, Psalms 127:2)

16. Angels are protecting and working on my behalf as I rest and sleep (Psalms 34:7, 91:11).
17. I decree that instead of demonic activity and hellish dreams, God instructs me in the night season (Psalm 16:7).
18. For it is God's desire for me to know the mysteries of the kingdom of heaven. I therefore declare that as I sleep, I shall not only awaken refreshed, but shall have prophetic dreams and visions and receive kingdom keys, strategies, and heavenly downloads from my God. These revelations shall expose the enemy, release answers, direction, cures, and understanding, change life, build faith, shift atmospheres, overtake regions, and produce and establish the glory of God in the earth (Matthew 13:11).
19. Even in my sleep, I take up the yoke of the Lord. Your yoke is comforting, delivering, healing, revitalizing, strengthening, empowering, elevating, activating and releasing fulfillment to my royal lineage and destiny (Matthew 11:28).
20. I shall arise proclaiming that my sleep was sweet, for I have been fruitfully blessed and nourished in sweet heavenly sleep (Jeremiah 31:26).

PEACE! Not As The World Gives

1. I the name of Jesus, decree that I receive my
    heavenly reality of unshakable peace from
    You, Jesus. Peace! Not as the world gives.
    But peace that comes from the very DNA of
    my heavenly home (John 14:27).
2. As a *Kingdom Heir,* I thank You for
    imparting Your peace into me, for leaving it
    with me, and for encouraging me to
    embrace the power, authority, aroma,
    nature and heavenly reality of peace.
3. I reject the trials and tribulations of this
    world. Even when challenging situations
    occur, I remain in a tranquil state of peace.
4. I continually seek You for my purposed
    destiny and I am open to walking out
    naturally what has already occurred in the
    spirit realm. I say burdens, oppression, and
    mental anguish are not my lot. And even
    when being persecuted for righteousness
    sake, I remained grounded in the purpose
    of my destiny. I remained consecrated in
    the vigor of peace.
5. For You, Christ Jesus have continuously
    reminded me and demonstrated through
    the fulfillment of Your work at the cross,
    that the world has been conquered. As a
    Kingdom Heir, I, too, have subdued,
    prevailed, overcome and conquered this
    world.
6. I am victorious and assert my victory! I
    decree I am more than conquerors through

Christ Jesus who loves us. *I am uncompromisingly persuaded beyond a doubt (am sure) that neither death nor life, nor angels nor principalities, nor things impending and threatening nor things to come, nor powers, nor height nor depth, nor anything else in all creation will be able to separate me from the love of God which is in Christ Jesus my Lord* (Romans 8:38-39).

7. Though the enemy devises his strategies, they are thwarted. He proposes his plans, yet they will not stand. I rebuke the strategies of the enemy while declaring exemption from rage of demonic havoc and war. I spew out peace!

8. God thwarts the plans of the crafty so that their hands achieve no success, for God is with me. He has given me complete, sound, surpassing peace. Such peace yields a state of security and order in my sphere of influence...harmonizing all that concerns me (Job 5:12, Isa 8:10).

9. Plan and plot all you want--nothing will prosper. All your talk is mere babble, empty words with no fruit; because when all is said and done, the last word is Immanuel--God-With-Us. He is my voice, my reality, my temperament, my peace.

10. Call your councils of war, but they will be worthless. Develop your strategies, but they will not succeed. For God is with me! I still myself in the call to trust the Lord, I still the storms of life with my validity of peace (Isa 8:10).

11. In Jesus name, I call forth a mutual concord of agreement between my heavenly government and the government of this world. I declare silence upon the hostilities that attempts to steal, destroy, dismantle and displace the calm felicity of my assertive peace.

12. For You Lord, have ordained, orchestrated, delegated, and declared the judgment and laws of my surroundings. I am established in Your peace (Isaiah 26:12).

13. You guard me and keep me in perfect and constant peace because my mind - both its inclination and its character – stays centered in You; I am committed to You, lean on You and hope confidently in You (Isaiah 26: 3).

14. Your peace is a fruitful weapon that proclaims my spiritual supremacy. It isn't conditional, flawed, empty or temporary, like the world gives. It is a silent vengeance evaporating the wretched storm. I declare Your supernatural gift of peace.

BAM The Devil Scriptures

Psalms 109:29 - *Let mine adversaries be clothed with shame, and let them cover themselves with their own confusion, as with a mantle.*

New Living Translation - *May my accusers be clothed with disgrace and wrapped in shame as in a cloak.*

The Message Version – *Let them be jeered by the crowd when they stand up, followed by cheers for me, your servant. Dress my accusers in clothes dirty with shame, discarded and humiliating old ragbag clothes.*

Psalm 35:26 - *May all who gloat over my distress be put to shame and confusion; may all who exalt themselves over me be clothed with shame and disgrace.*

Psalm 109:18 - *He wore cursing as his garment; it entered into his body like water, into his bones like oil.*

Psalms 109:17-20 - *Yes, he loved cursing, and it came [back] upon him; he delighted not in blessing, and it was far from him. He clothed himself also with cursing as with his garment, and it seeped into his inward [life] like water, and like oil into his bones. Let it be to him as the raiment with which he covers himself and as the girdle with which he is girded continually. Let this be the reward of my adversaries from the Lord, and of those who speak evil against my life.*

As he loved cursing, so let it come unto him: as he delighted not in blessing, so let it be far from him. As he clothed himself with cursing like as with his garment, so let it come into his bowels like water, and like oil into his bones. Let it be unto him as the garment which covereth him, and for a girdle (belt, strength) wherewith he is girded continually. Let this be the reward of mine adversaries from the Lord, and of them that speak evil against my soul

Psalms 40:13-15 - *Be pleased, O Lord, to deliver (defend, rescue) me: O Lord, make haste to help me. Let them be ashamed and confounded (embarrassed, reproached) together that seek after my soul to destroy it; let them be driven backward and put to shame that wish me evil. Let them be desolate for a reward of their shame (confusion) that say unto me, Aha, aha.*

Desolate is "samem" in the Hebrew and means *"to be desolate, be appalled, stun, stupefy, horrored, horror-causer, deflowered, ravaged, astounded, ruined."*

Psalms 35:4-12 – *Let them be confounded (delayed, disconcerted) and put to shame that seek after my soul: let them be turned back and brought to confusion that devise my hurt. Let them be as chaff (driven out, rubbish, waste) before the wind: and let the angel of the Lord chase them. Let their way be dark (miserable) and slippery (treacherous): and let the angel of the Lord persecute them. For without cause have they hid for me their net in a pit (destruction,*

176

corruption, a grave), which without cause they have digged for my soul.

Let destruction come upon him at unawares; and let his net (is reset in the Hebrew and means trap or judgment) that he hath hid catch himself: into that very destruction let him fall. And my soul shall be joyful in the Lord: it shall rejoice in his salvation. All my bones shall say, Lord, who is like unto thee, which deliverest the poor from him that is too strong for him, yea, the poor and the needy from him that spoileth him? False witnesses did rise up; they laid to my charge things that I knew not. They rewarded me evil for good to the spoiling of my soul.

Psalm 63:9 *- Those who want to kill me will be destroyed; they will go down to the depths of the earth.*

Psalm 71:13 *- May my accusers perish in shame; may those who want to harm me be covered with scorn and disgrace.*

Psalm 119:95 *- The wicked are waiting to destroy me, but I will ponder your statutes.*

Psalms 60:12 *- Through God we will do valiantly, for it is He who shall tread down our enemies.*

Psalms 125:3 *- For the scepter of wickedness shall not rest on the land allotted to the righteous, lest the righteous reach out their hands to iniquity."*

Psalms **27:5-6** - *For in the time of trouble He shall hide me in His pavilion; in the secret place of His tabernacle He shall hide me; He shall set me high upon a rock. And now my head shall be lifted up above my enemies all around me; therefore I will offer sacrifices of joy in His tabernacle; I will sing, yes, I will sing praises to the Lord.*

Jeremiah **14:3** - *The nobles send their servants for water; they go to the cisterns but find no water. They return with their jars unfilled; dismayed and despairing, they cover their heads.*

Job **8:20** - *They that hate thee shall be clothed with shame; and the dwelling place of the wicked shall come to nought.*

Deuteronomy **28:7** - *The Lord will cause your enemies who rise against you to be defeated before your face; they shall come out against you one way and flee before you seven ways.*

Isaiah **54:17** - *No weapon formed against you shall prosper, and every tongue which rises against you in judgment you shall condemn. This is the heritage of the servants of the Lord, and their righteousness is from Me," Says the Lord.*

Isaiah **41:11-12** - *Behold, all those who were incensed against you shall be ashamed and disgraced; they shall be as nothing, And those who strive with you shall perish. You shall seek them and not find them - Those who contended* *with you. Those who war against you shall be as nothing, as a nonexistent thing.*

1John 4:4 - You, dear children, are from God and have overcome them, because the one who is in you is greater than the one who is in the world.

Luke 10:19 - I have given you authority to trample on snakes and scorpions and to overcome all the power of the enemy; nothing will harm you.

Romans 16:20 - The God of peace will soon crush Satan under your feet. The grace of our Lord Jesus be with you.

Romans 8:37-39 - No, in all these things we are more than conquerors through him who loved us. For I am convinced that neither death nor life, neither angels nor demons . . . will be able to separate us from the love of God that is in Christ Jesus our Lord.

James 4:7 - Submit yourselves, then, to God. Resist the devil, and he will flee from you.

1John 3:8 . . . The reason the Son of God appeared was to destroy the devil's work.

Mark 6:7 . . . Calling the Twelve to him, he sent them out two by two and gave them authority over evil spirits.

Luke 10:17 - *The seventy-two returned with joy and said, "Lord, even the demons submit to us in your name."*

Matthew 16:19 - *I will give you the keys of the kingdom of heaven; whatever you bind on earth will be bound in heaven, and whatever you loose on earth will be loosed in heaven.*

Matthew 28:18 - *Then Jesus came to them and said, "All authority in heaven and on earth has been given to me. Therefore go. . . ."*

John 14:12 - *I tell you the truth, anyone who has faith in me will do what I have been doing. He will do even greater things than these, because I am going to the Father.*

Malachi 4:3 - *And you shall tread down the wicked; for they shall be ashes under the soles of your feet in the day that I shall do this, saith the Lord of hosts.*

Sieging Your Enemy!

This is a revelation the Lord released during a time when the enemy was striving to rage war with things that could not be a part of the season Kingdom Shifters Ministries was entering into. Sieges will be necessary in these times, during situations where you will need to take a prophetic stance against the enemy, and in certain times of warfare and intercession.

Declaration!
We set an eternal siege against everything that cannot go with us into the next season or cannot be a part of our current situation! Let our siege be a sign that we have shifted to a new fortified FEARLESS place in God! SIEGE & SHIFT!

Ezekiel 2:3-4 - And lay siege against it, and build a fort against it, and cast a mount against it; set the camp also against it, and set battering rams against it round about. Moreover take thou unto thee an iron pan, and set it for a wall of iron between thee and the city: and set thy face against it, and it shall be besieged, and thou shalt lay siege against it. This shall be a sign to the house of Israel.

Lay Siege against it (call them or the situations by name)!

Dictionary.com defines *"siege"* as *"a military operation in which enemy forces surround a town or building, cutting off essential supplies, with the aim of compelling the surrender of those inside."*

<u>*Siege* is *"masar"* in the Hebrew and means:</u>
1. besieged, bulwark, defense, fenced, fortress
2. strong (hold), tower, enclosure, entrenchment

Build a fort against it!

<u>Dictionary.com defines *fort* as:</u>
1. a strong or fortified place occupied by troops and usually surrounded by walls, ditches, and other defensive works
2. a fortress, fortification
3. any permanent army post, (formerly) a trading post

A *fort* is *"daeyq"* in the Hebrew and is defined as *"a battering- tower, bulwark, siege-wall, sidewall."*

Cast a mount against it!

<u>Dictionary.com defines *"mount"* as:</u>
1. to attach to or fix on or in a support, backing, setting, etc.
2. to arrange for display, to organize
3. to prepare and launch, as an attack or a campaign
4. to raise or put into position for use, as a gun

182

Mount in the Hebrew is *"cowllah"* and means, *"a military mound, i. e. rampart of besiegers, bank, mount."*

Set a camp against it!

Dictionary.com defines *"camp"* as:
1. a place where an army or other group of persons or an individual is lodged in a tent or tents or other temporary means of shelter
2. any position in which ideals, doctrines, a group of troops, workers, etc., camping and moving together

Camp in the Hebrew is *"mahaneh"* and means:
1. encampment (of travelers or troops)
2. hence, an army, whether literal (of soldiers) or figurative (of dancers, angels, cattle, locusts, stars; or even the sacred courts)
3. army, band, battle, camp, company, drove, host, tents.

The camp consist of angels, the saints/warriors, clouds of witness

Set a battering rams against it round about!

Battering Rams is *"kar"* in the Hebrew and means:
1. the sense of plumpness; a ram (as full-grown and fat), including a battering- ram (as butting)

2. hence, a meadow (as for sheep), also a pad or camel's saddle (as puffed out)
3. captain, furniture, lamb, (large) pasture, ram.

Dictionary.com defines *"battering ram"* as:
1. an ancient military device with a heavy horizontal ram for battering down walls, gates, etc.
2. any of various similar devices, usually machine-powered, used in demolition, by police and firefighters to force entrance to a building, etc.

With the battering rams being set up round about, the enemy is continually being hit from every side.

Set it for a wall of iron between thee and the city!

Dictionary.com defines *"iron"* as:
1. something hard, strong, rigid, unyielding, or the like, hearts of iron
2. an instrument, utensil, weapon, etc., made of iron, a sword
3. strong, robust; healthy
4. holding or binding strongly: an iron grip

Iron is a symbolism of armor. *Iron* represents is hard so it also represents harshness...a hard stance.

Set thy face against it! Set up face! WHEWWWW!

Face in the Hebrew is *"paniym"* *"the face (as the part that turns); beseech, countenance, edge, employ, endure."*

Besiege it!

Besiege in the Hebrew is *"masor"* or *"matsuwr"* and means:
1. something hemming in, i. e. (objectively) a mound (of besiegers)
2. (abstractly) a siege, (figuratively) distress; or (subjectively) a fastness
3. besieged, bulwark, defense, fenced, fortress, siege, strong (hold), tower. entrenchment, siege works

Dictionary.com defines *"besiege"* as:
1. to lay siege to
2. to crowd around; crowd in upon; surround
3. to assail or ply, as with requests or demands

I hear lay hold of it! It will be a sign!

Sign is *"ot"* in the Hebrew and means, *"a flag, beacon, monument, prodigy, evidence, signal a distinguishing mark banner remembrance miraculous sign omen warning token, ensign, standard, miracle, proof."*

This sign should be proof to the nations of what God does, who God is.

A siege is requires strategizing and positioning. A siege is about strategizing a

185

plan, then standing in your authority of consistently implementing that plan until you have become the capturer rather than the captive.

In a siege you control the hardship, sin, warfare, harasser, etc. instead of it controlling you. You do this by setting up and implementing a strategy where you take that enemy hostage. You cut off every way he can feast on and in your life and/or situation. You then besiege the enemy by not surrendering that thing until it gives up on harassing your life.

The Message Version - Then make a model of a military siege against the brick: Build siege walls, construct a ramp, set up army camps, lay in battering rams around it. Then get an iron skillet and place it upright between you and the city--an iron wall. Face the model: The city shall be under siege and you shall be the besieger. This is a sign to the family of Israel.

New English Translation - Lay siege to it! Build siege works against it. Erect a siege ramp against it! Post soldiers outside it and station battering rams around it. Then for your part take an iron frying pan and set it up as an iron wall between you and the city. Set your face toward it. It is to be under siege; you are to besiege it. This is a sign for the house of Israel.

New Living Translation - Show the city under siege. Build a wall around it so no one can escape. Set up the enemy camp, and surround the city with siege ramps and battering rams. Then take an iron griddle and place it between you and the city. Turn toward the city and demonstrate how harsh the siege will be against Jerusalem. This will be a warning to the people of Israel.

Entering True Rest

I am adding this section because it is important for a prayer warrior to know when to rest and when God is calling them to rest. Be obedient during seasons of rests, this will diminish unnecessary warfare and persecution and enable the warrior to rest and refresh for the next season of reigning.

Hebrews 4:11 - Let us labour therefore to enter into that rest, lest any - man fall after the same example of unbelief.

Labour is "spoudazo" in the Greek and means:
1. seed (used in sowing): to use speed, i. e. to make effort, be prompt or earnest
2. do (give) diligence, be diligent (forward), endeavor, labour, study
3. be forward, labour, study, to hasten, make haste, to exert one's self

The Greek word for *labour* denotes that when we are diligent to enter a place of rest in God, it is seed used for sowing. We sow in being diligent to rest, and God rewards us by doing or leading us in doing all the work that needs to be done in us and for us. We are totally submitted to His strength and His Spirit and do nothing of and in our own accord.

It is therefore important to have a passion in staying in this place when God is requiring
188

it of us. We are to pursue it with passion as we would pursue anything that we deem important. We are also to be okay with ceasing from works, personal pulls, and pulls of people or obligations and responsibilities that will only drain and steal our time of renewal in God.

Rest is _"katapausis"_ in the Greek and means:
1. reposing down, i. e. (by Hebraism) abode
2. a putting to rest calming of the winds, a resting place
3. metaphor: the heavenly blessedness in which God dwells, and of which he has promised to make persevering believers in Christ partakers after the toils and trials of life on earth are ended.

Dictionary.com defines _"repose"_ as:
1. to lie at rest
2. to lie dead <reposing in state>
3. to remain still or concealed
4. to take a rest, rely
5. to rest for support: lie

As we are diligent in pursuing such a place of rest and calmness, our spiritual and natural posture should literally appear as dead. Also things should die in us just because we have been obedient to resting in God.

Repose suggests that this rest should be as a death. The quietness we enter should be in such submission that we appear dead from

189

doing works and totally submitted and focused in being humbled, bowed and prostrate before Jesus.

The New Living Translation of Hebrews 4:12 says:

For the word of God is living and active and sharper than any double- edged sword, piercing even to the point of dividing soul from spirit, and joints from marrow; it is able to judge the desires and thoughts of the heart. And no creature is hidden from God, but everything is naked and exposed to the eyes of him to whom we must render an account.

This asserts that we are not trying to hide our sins and faults but are taking them to God - before him. As we are diligent in resting, His word goes in and surgically removes everything that is not like Him. It divides the good from the bad and cleanses us (our souls), while renewing and reconnecting us (our spirits) in places that were disconnected from Him.

The Message Version of Verse 12

God means what he says. What he says goes. His powerful Word is sharp as a surgeon's scalpel, cutting through everything, whether doubt or defense, laying us open to listen and obey. Nothing and no one is impervious to God's Word. We can't get away from it--no matter what.

The Amplified Versions of Verse 11-12
*Let us therefore be zealous and exert ourselves
and strive diligently to enter that rest [of God, to
know and experience it for ourselves], that no
one may fall or perish by the same kind of
unbelief and disobedience [into which those in
the wilderness fell]. For the Word that God
speaks is alive and full of power [making it
active, operative, energizing, and effective]; it is
sharper than any two- edged sword, penetrating
to the dividing line of the breath of life (soul) and
[the immortal] spirit, and of joints and marrow
[of the deepest parts of our nature], exposing and
sifting and analyzing and judging the very
thoughts and purposes of the heart.*

<u>*Sharper* is "*tomoteros*" in the Greek and
means</u>:
1. comparative of a derivative of the primary
   temno (to cut; more comprehensive or
   decisive than, as if by a single stroke
   whereas that implies repeated blows, like
   hacking)
2. more keen, sharper

Resting Prayer
We diligently seek to rest in you God. We
repent for anyway we have not rested when
you required it and we shift to diligently
pursuing a resting place of refuge in you.
 As we rest Lord, let your word take refuge
in us. Go deep in releasing your word in us
Lord.

191

Let the sharp scalpel of your word
surgically work in us Jesus! We willingly
come to the operation table of rest to be
judged by your word, to be delivered by
your word, to be healed by your word, to be
revived by your word, to be renewed by
your word, to be refreshed by your word,
and to be further directed by your word.

Lord divide and separate us from
everything that is not like you. Disconnect
and gut out everything that does not look
like or portray you. Penetrate deeply -
pierce deeply where we are gutted out to
the very foundation of our existence.

Everything that cannot go into the next
season, we say scalpel it out Father. Let the
sword be keen in discerning and removing
all evil, all the demonic, every crevice and
fashion of the devil and his existence.

And as you do a complete work in us, as we
die in you. Conceal your likeness in us
Jesus. Reconnect us to you in places we
have been detached. Reconnect us in places
where we have been damaged due to past
warfare, sin, or illegal violations of the
enemy.

Ohhhhh!!! We die in you and rise in you
Jesus. We die on your operation table of
rest and rise into resurrection newness in
you Jesus.

192

Yes! Yes! Yes! We take our rest and let you do you in us Jesus. We submit to the work that only you can do in this time of dying in your secret place of rest.

References:
The Holy Bible in different versions
Dictionary.com
Merriam Webster's Online Dictionary
Strong's Concordance

Cover Design and Layout:

Book Picture Cover is by James Parks and layout design
by Reenita Keys
Connect with them via Facebook

Kingdom Shifters Books & Apparel
Available at Kingdomshifters.com

195

Made in the USA
Coppell, TX
18 December 2023